SQL

THE ULTIMATE GUIDE FROM BEGINNER TO EXPERT – LEARN AND MASTER SQL IN NO TIME!

BY: PETER ADAMS

TABLE OF CONTENTS

INTRODUCTION

Congratulations on making it to the summary of the most interesting,

knowledge filled, all-encompassing book on SQL available today. Not only will this book amaze you with the amount of knowledge and reference it provides, it will also guide you through the process of learning the language, functions, and statements involved in the process. This ultimate guide to SQL will take you from beginner status to expert level by the time you reach the conclusion.

CHAPTER 1

THE FUNDAMENTALS OF SQL

These days, data has become one of the most important areas of study and work. In fact, the digital world revolves around data completely. Services such as Facebook and Google have all been made possible because of the acute need of data. These companies gather data from their users and provide them to marketers and advertisers. In turn, the marketers make use of the data to develop marketing strategies and campaigns that attract their customers more effectively.

The above is just one example of the important role played by data in our society. Now, simply having data is not enough. You need to be able to manage it in an effective manner as well. For that, you need an excellent database management system.

This is where SQL comes in. It is widely considered to be one of the most popular database engines. Let's take a detailed look at it shall we?

SQL: An Introduction

The term SQL is short for Structured Query Language. This is a computer language that is used for storing, retrieving and manipulating the data kept in a relational database. We will take a look at relational databases shortly. When it comes to relation database systems, the standard language used is SQL. In fact, all relational database systems such as MS Access, MySQL, Oracle and Sybase make use of SQL as their standard language.

However, these systems use their own dialects of the language. Take a look at some of them below.

- T-SQL is used by MS SQL Server

- PL/SQL is used Oracle

- JET SQL is the version of SQL used by MS Access

Understanding the SQL Process

Before we proceed any further, it is a good idea to become familiar with the SQL process. When an SQL command is being executed, the system, irrespective of the RDBMS being used, will determine the best way for carrying out the request. The SQL engine will determine how the task is going to be interpreted.

Several components are present in the process. Some of the components are Optimization Engines, Query Dispatcher, SQL Query Engine and Classic Query Engine. The classic query engine will handle all the non-SQL queries. However, the SQL query engine is not going to handle the logical files.

Why use SQL?

There are several reasons as to why SQL is used by database systems. Let's go through some of those reasons here.

- SQL enables the data to be described by the users.

- It allows the data stored in relational database management systems to be accessed by the users.

- Users can define the data stored in a database and even manipulate the data with the SQL.

- SQL enables it to be embedded inside other languages with the help of SQL libraries, pre-compilers and modules.

- Users will be able to create databases and tables and drop them.

- Users can use SQL to create functions, views and procedures in the database.

- SQL allows the users to define and set permissions on procedures, tables and views.

A Short History of SQL

SQL is quite old. Its origins can be traced all the way back to 1970. In 1970, a relational model of databases was described by Dr. Edgar F. Codd while working at IBM. He is often referred to as the father of relational databases. However, it was not until 1974 that SQL actually appeared. Using the ideas of Codd, IBM began to work on such a system resulting in the creation of System/R which was released in 1978.

Relational Software, Inc. also realized the potential of the ideas laid down by Codd and began to work on those concepts. The company, which would later come to be called Oracle Corporation, released the Oracle V2 in 1979. This was the first implementation of SQL that was available commercially.

Finally in 1986, the first prototype of a relational database system was developed by IBM. ANSI standardized it as well.

RDBMS: An Introduction

RDBMS is simply the abbreviation for Relational Database Management System. It is the foundation on which SQL has been created. In fact, it serves as the basis for all the modern database systems including Oracle, MS SQL Server, Microsoft Access and MySQL. In simple terms, RDBMS is a type of database management system which has been established upon the relational model that was conceptualized by Dr. Codd.

The Concepts

There are several concepts in RDBMS that you should become familiar with. They are the fundamentals to learning SQL and, as such, are crucial to your progress.

What is a Table?

In any RDBMS, the data is stored inside database objects which are known as tables. A table can be defined as a collection of data entries that are related. A table is made up of columns and rows. The table is the simplest and most common type of data storage available in a relational database. Take a look at the following example of a table called EMPLOYEES.

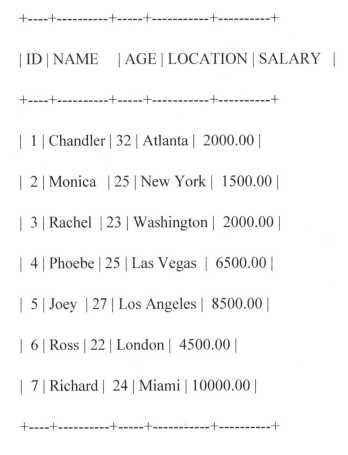

```
+----+----------+-----+-----------+----------+
| ID | NAME     | AGE | LOCATION  | SALARY   |
+----+----------+-----+-----------+----------+
|  1 | Chandler | 32  | Atlanta   | 2000.00  |
|  2 | Monica   | 25  | New York  | 1500.00  |
|  3 | Rachel   | 23  | Washington| 2000.00  |
|  4 | Phoebe   | 25  | Las Vegas | 6500.00  |
|  5 | Joey     | 27  | Los Angeles| 8500.00 |
|  6 | Ross     | 22  | London    | 4500.00  |
|  7 | Richard  | 24  | Miami     | 10000.00 |
+----+----------+-----+-----------+----------+
```

What is a Field?

All tables are divided into smaller components known as fields. In the example given above, the fields of the EMPLOYEES table are ID, AGE, Name, Salary and Location. In other words, a column which has been designed for maintaining specific information on all the records in the table is known as a field.

What is a Record?

Also known as a row, a record is the individual entry present inside a table. In other words, a record is simply a horizontal entity present in a table. In the example given above, the EMPLOYEES table has a total of 7 records. Given below is one single record from the table.

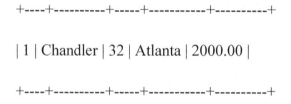

```
+----+----------+-----+-----------+----------+
| 1 | Chandler | 32 | Atlanta | 2000.00 |
+----+----------+-----+-----------+----------+
```

What is a Column?

While horizontal entities are referred to as records, vertical entities are known as columns. A column will have all the information that is related to a particular field in the table. In the EMPLOYEES table, one of the columns is NAME. This column represents the names.

```
+-----------+
| ADDRESS |
+-----------+
```

| Chandler |

| Monica |

| Rachel |

| Phoebe |

| Joey |

| Ross |

| Richard |

+----+------+

What is a NULL value?

In a table, a NULL value is the value of a field which is blank. In other words, there are no values whatsoever in a NULL value field. You must remember that a NULL value is not at all equal to a zero value. Fields which contain spaces do not have a NULL value as well. Instead, NULL value denotes that the field has been left blank when the record was being created.

What are SQL Constraints?

Constraints are the rules which regulate the data columns present in a table. They can limit the kind of data which can be inserted into a table. Constraints help in increasing the reliability and accuracy of the data present in the database. Constraints can be either column level or the table level. Constraints in the column level will be applied to just a single column. However, constraints of the table level will be applied to the entire table.

The constraints which are available and commonly used in SQL are discussed as follows.

DEFAULT Constraint: This assigns a default value to a column. When no value is specified by the user, the default value will be used.

NOT NULL Constraint: This ensures that NULL value cannot be used in the column.

UNIQUE Constraint: This constraint is used for making sure that the same values cannot be used in a column. In other words, all the values will be different from each other.

PRIMARY Key: This is the unique identifier for each of the records present in the table.

FOREIGN Key: This is the unique identifier for a record in another table of the same database.

CHECK Constraint: This is used for ensuring that certain conditions are satisfied by the values present in the column.

INDEX: This used for creating and retrieving data from a database quickly.

Understanding Data Integrity

Data integrity, as the name suggests, is about the overall accuracy, consistency and completeness of the data. Integrity can be indicated by the lack of alterations between the two updates or instances of a record. In other words, the data is unchanged and intact. Data integrity will be typically enforced as the database is being designed by means of standard rules and procedures. It is possible to maintain data integrity with different error analysis methods as well as validation procedures.

Data integrity will be imposed in relational database models as well as hierarchical database models. In the case of relational database models, data integrity is ensured by the use of the following integrity constraints.

Entity Integrity: Entity integrity is related to the concept of primary keys. As per this rule, each table should have its very own primary key. Each key should be completely unique and not be null.

Referential Integrity: Referential integrity deals with the foreign keys concept. As per this constraint, the value of a foreign key can exist in two states. In the first state, the foreign key value will be a reference to the value of the primary key of another table. The second state is null. This means that no relationships exist or that the relationship is not known.

Domain Integrity: As per this constraint, all the columns present in a relational database will be in a defined domain.

User-Defined Integrity: This constraint imposes some specific rules which cannot be classified under any of the other types of data integrity. As the name suggests, they are defined by the user.

Understanding Database Normalization

A database must be usable. For that to happen, the data present in it must be organized properly. The process by which the data is efficiently organized in the database is known as database normalization. There are 2 reasons why database normalization is necessary.

- It results in the elimination of redundant data. An example of redundant data would be storing the exact same data in multiple tables.

- It ensures that the data dependencies are sensible.

These are important aims as they end up decreasing the amount of space required by a database. At the same time, they ensure that there is logic in the way data is stored. Database normalization involves a range of guidelines which help in the creation of an excellent database structure.

The guidelines for normalization are separated into normal forms. A normal form is the way or the format in which the database structure is determined. Normal forms help in the organization of the database structure and ensure that it is in compliance with the rules applicable for the first normal form, followed by the second normal form and then the third normal form. There are more normal forms. However, the third normal form is going to be enough for now.

Let us take a look at each below.

First Normal Form

Also known as 1NF, this sets the most fundamental rules that an organized database should follow. Those rules are.

- The data items necessary should be defined as they will be the columns in the table. Data items which are related should be stored in a table.

- There should not be any repetitions in the groups of data.

- A primary key must always be present.

Second Normal Form

Also known as 2NF, the second normal form declares that all rules for the first normal form should be met. Additionally, there should not be any partial dependences of any column on the primary key.

Third Normal Form

Also known as 3NF, the third normal form is said to have been achieved when the conditions given below have been met.

- The second normal form has been achieved by the table.

- The primary key is depended upon by all the non-primary fields. The dependency of the non-primary fields takes place between data.

These are the major fundamentals that you should become familiar with when you are getting started with SQL. There will be certainly a lot more to learn in the coming chapters. However, knowing the above points will make it easier to make progress in learning SQL.

CHAPTER 2

THE SYNTAX OF SQL

Like all computer languages, SQL, too, is governed by a set of guidelines and rules as to how the commands are to be used. You will learn about the syntax of basic SQL commands in this chapter.

There are standards in place that enable SQL to be usable in different databases. Despite the presence of standards, SQL code is unable to enjoy complete portability among the various database systems. Instead, adjustments are necessary to make the code accessible in various databases.

On the other hand, there are certain features which remain applicable irrespective of the database using the code. All statements in SQL will need to start with any one of the following keywords.

- SELECT

- UPDATE

- INSERT

- ALTER

- DELETE

- CREATE

- DROP

- SHOW

- USE

Another important point you must note is that there is no case sensitivity in SQL. Therefore, 'INSERT' and 'insert' will have the same result in a SQL Statement. On the other hand, MySQL will recognize case sensitivity for the table names. You need to remember this point when you are working in MySQL.

Language Elements in SQL

There are quite a few elements in SQL. Knowing and understanding them will be essential to getting a good grip on the language.

Clauses: These are the elemental components of queries and statements. They can be optional in certain cases.

Expressions: These components are capable of producing scalar values. Alternatively, they can also produce tables that contain rows and columns of data.

Predicates: These elements can specific the conditions which can be evaluated as per the three-valued logic of SQL. As per this logic, known in short as 3VL, there are only three values possible: true, false or unknown. They are used for limiting the effects of queries and statements. Alternatively, they can be used for changing the program flow.

Queries: Queries are responsible for retrieving the data based on the criteria specified. They are one of the most important elements in SQL.

Statements: They may be used for having a constant effect on data and schemata. Alternatively, they may be used for controlling program flow, transactions, sessions, diagnostics or connections.

In SQL, a statement must also include a semicolon to denote that the statement has been terminated. While this is not necessary for all platforms, it is a standard rule in SQL syntax.

Insignificant whitespace will typically be ignored when present in queries and statements in SQL. This makes it easier to format the code in SQL to enhance readability.

The following illustrates the syntax for a range of common elements in SQL. Note this table as it will be a useful quick reference guide when you are working on your own SQL code.

SQL Statement	Syntax
AND / OR	SELECT column_name(s) FROM table_name WHERE condition AND|OR condition
ALTER TABLE	ALTER TABLE table_name ADD column_name datatype or ALTER TABLE table_name DROP COLUMN column_name
AS (alias)	SELECT column_name AS column_alias FROM table_name or SELECT column_name FROM table_name AS table_alias
BETWEEN	SELECT column_name(s) FROM table_name WHERE column_name BETWEEN value1 AND value2
CREATE DATABASE	CREATE DATABASE database_name
CREATE TABLE	CREATE TABLE table_name (column_name1 data_type, column_name2 data_type, column_name3 data_type, ...)
CREATE INDEX	CREATE INDEX index_name ON table_name (column_name) or CREATE UNIQUE INDEX index_name ON table_name (column_name)
CREATE VIEW	CREATE VIEW view_name AS SELECT column_name(s) FROM table_name WHERE condition
DELETE	DELETE FROM table_name WHERE some_column=some_value or DELETE FROM table_name

	(Note: Deletes the entire table!!)
	DELETE * FROM table_name
	(Note: Deletes the entire table!!)
DROP DATABASE	DROP DATABASE database_name
DROP INDEX	DROP INDEX table_name.index_name (SQL Server)
	DROP INDEX index_name ON table_name (MS Access)
	DROP INDEX index_name (DB2/Oracle)
	ALTER TABLE table_name
	DROP INDEX index_name (MySQL)
DROP TABLE	DROP TABLE table_name
EXISTS	IF EXISTS (SELECT * FROM table_name WHERE id = ?)
	BEGIN
	--do what needs to be done if exists
	END
	ELSE
	BEGIN
	--do what needs to be done if not
	END
IN	SELECT column_name, aggregate_function(column_name)
	FROM table_name
	WHERE column_name operator value
	GROUP BY column_name
	SELECT column_name(s)
	FROM table_name
	WHERE column_name
	IN (value1,value2,..)
HAVING	SELECT column_name, aggregate_function(column_name)
	FROM table_name
	WHERE column_name operator value
	GROUP BY column_name
	HAVING aggregate_function(column_name) operator value
GROUP BY	SELECT column_name, aggregate_function(column_name)
	FROM table_name
	WHERE column_name operator value
	GROUP BY column_name

INSERT INTO	INSERT INTO table_name VALUES (value1, value2, value3,....) or INSERT INTO table_name (column1, column2, column3,...) VALUES (value1, value2, value3,....)
INNER JOIN	SELECT column_name(s) FROM table_name1 INNER JOIN table_name2 ON table_name1.column_name=table_name2.column_name
LEFT JOIN	SELECT column_name(s) FROM table_name1 LEFT JOIN table_name2 ON table_name1.column_name=table_name2.column_name
RIGHT JOIN	SELECT column_name(s) FROM table_name1 RIGHT JOIN table_name2 ON table_name1.column_name=table_name2.column_name
FULL JOIN	SELECT column_name(s) FROM table_name1 FULL JOIN table_name2 ON table_name1.column_name=table_name2.column_name
LIKE	SELECT column_name(s) FROM table_name WHERE column_name LIKE pattern
ORDER BY	SELECT column_name(s) FROM table_name ORDER BY column_name [ASC|DESC]
SELECT	SELECT column_name(s) FROM table_name
SELECT *	SELECT * FROM table_name
SELECT DISTINCT	SELECT DISTINCT column_name(s) FROM table_name
SELECT INTO	SELECT * INTO new_table_name [IN externaldatabase] FROM old_table_name or SELECT column_name(s) INTO new_table_name [IN externaldatabase] FROM old_table_name

SELECT TOP	SELECT TOP number|percent column_name(s)
	FROM table_name
TRUNCATE TABLE	TRUNCATE TABLE table_name
UNION	SELECT column_name(s) FROM table_name1
	UNION
	SELECT column_name(s) FROM table_name2
UNION ALL	SELECT column_name(s) FROM table_name1
	UNION ALL
	SELECT column_name(s) FROM table_name2
UPDATE	UPDATE table_name
	SET column1=value, column2=value,...
	WHERE some_column=some_value
WHERE	SELECT column_name(s)
	FROM table_name
	WHERE column_name operator value

You need to become familiar with the syntax of SQL if you want to become capable of writing your own code. It is fundamental to your success in this language. As such, you must keep working on strengthening your foundation in the syntax. Getting the syntax incorrect is bound to have an impact on your code, making it completely unusable. You may end up spending hours correcting the syntax. Go through the chapter again if you have any doubts. Keep working on the syntax and make it a second habit.

CHAPTER 3

DATA TYPES IN SQL

Data is at the core of SQL. After all, SQL was created to make it easier to manipulate the data stored inside a database. It ensures that you do not have to sort through large chunks of data manually in search of what you want. Now, there are various types of data that can be stored in the database depending on the platform used. As such, you now need to learn about the data types available in SQL.

Data Types: An Introduction

The data type specifies the kind of data which can be stored in a column of a database table. When creating a table, it is important to decide the data type which is going to be used for defining the columns. Data types can also be used for defining variables and for storing procedure output and input parameters. The data type will instruct SQL to expect a particular kind of data in each column.

A data type must be selected for each variable or column which is appropriate for the kind of data which is to be stored in that column or variable. Additionally, storage requirements must be considered. You need to select data types which ensure efficiency in the storage.

Selecting the correct data type for the variables, tables and stored procedures will improve the performance greatly as it will ensure that the execution plan is correct. At the same time, it will be a great improvement on data integrity as it ensures that the right data has been stored inside a database.

The List of Data Types

There are several data types used in SQL. The following table lists all of them along with a short description of what they are. Mark this table as it will prove to be invaluable as a reference guide on data types when you are learning and even later.

Before you start, you should take a moment to understand what precision and scale are. Precision is the total number of digits that is present in a number. Scale is the total number of digits located on the right side of the decimal point of a number. In the case of a number like 123.4567, the precision is 7 while the scale is 4.

INTEGER (p)	Integer numerical (no decimal). Precision p
SMALLINT	Integer numerical (no decimal). Precision 5
INTEGER	Integer numerical (no decimal). Precision 10
BIGINT	Integer numerical (no decimal). Precision 19
DECIMAL (p,s)	Exact numerical, precision p, scale s. Example: decimal(5,2) is a number that has 3 digits before the decimal and 2 digits after the decimal
NUMERIC (p,s)	Exact numerical, precision p, scale s. (Same as DECIMAL)
FLOAT(p)	Approximate numerical, mantissa precision p. A floating number in base 10 exponential notation. The size argument for this type consists of a single number specifying the minimum precision
REAL	Approximate numerical, mantissa precision 7
FLOAT	Approximate numerical, mantissa precision 16
DOUBLE PRECISION	Approximate numerical, mantissa precision 16
DATE	Stores year, month, and day values

TIME	Stores hour, minute, and second values
TIMESTAMP	Stores year, month, day, hour, minute, and second values
INTERVAL	Composed of a number of integer fields, representing a period of time, depending on the type of interval
ARRAY	A set-length and ordered collection of elements
MULTISET	A variable-length and unordered collection of elements
XML	Stores XML data

Variations among Database Platforms

The data types given above are common to all database platforms. However, there are some which are known by different names in different database platforms. This can be a source of confusion. As such, take a look at the variations in the table given below.

Data Type	Access	SQLServer	Oracle	MySQL	PostgreSQL
boolean	Yes/No	Bit	Byte	N/A	Boolean
integer	Number (integer)	Int	Number	Int Integer	Int Integer
float	Number (single)	Float Real	Number	Float	Numeric
currency	Currency	Money	N/A	N/A	Money
string (fixed)	N/A	Char	Char	Char	Char
string (variable)	Text (<256) Memo (65k+)	Varchar	Varchar	Varchar Varchar 2	Varchar
binary object	OLE Object Memo	Binary (fixed up to 8K) Varbinary (<8K) Image (<2GB)	Long Raw	Blob Text	Binary Varbinary

Data Types for Different Databases

Each database platform tends to have its own range of data types. As such, you need to know what those data types are in order to use those platforms effectively. Here, we shall be focusing on the most popular database platforms: MySQL, SQL Server and Microsoft Access. A short description has been provided with each data type.

Data Types in Microsoft Access

Data Type	Description
Text	Use for text or combinations of text and numbers. 255 characters' maximum
Memo	Memo is used for larger amounts of text. Stores up to 65,536 characters. Note: You cannot sort a memo field. However, they are searchable
Byte	Allows whole numbers from 0 to 255. Storage is 1 byte.
Integer	Allows whole numbers between -32,768 and 32,767. Storage is 2 bytes.
Long	Allows whole numbers between -2,147,483,648 and 2,147,483,647. Storage is 4 bytes.
Single	Single precision floating-point. Will handle most decimals. Storage is 4 bytes.
Double	Double precision floating-point. Will handle most decimals. Storage is 8 bytes.
Currency	Use for currency. Holds up to 15 digits of whole dollars, plus 4 decimal places. Tip: You can choose which country's currency to use. Storage is 8 bytes.
AutoNumber	AutoNumber fields automatically give each record its own number, usually starting at 1. Storage is 4 bytes.
Data/Time	Use for dates and times. Storage is 8 bytes.
Yes/No	A logical field can be displayed as Yes/No, True/False, or On/Off. In code, use the constants True and False (equivalent to -1 and 0). Note: Null values are not allowed in Yes/No fields. Storage is 1 bit.
Ole Object	Can store pictures, audio, video, or other BLOBs (Binary Large OBjects). Storage is up to 1GB.
Hyperlink	Contain links to other files, including web pages.
Lookup Wizard	Let you type a list of options, which can then be chosen from a drop-down list. Storage is 4 bytes

Data Types in MySQL

In MySQL, the data types available can be widely classified into 3 categories. They are text, date/time and number. We shall take a look at the available data types in each category in the following tables.

MySQL Data Types

Data Type (Text)	Description
CHAR(size)	Holds a fixed length string (can contain letters, numbers, and special characters). The fixed size is specified in parenthesis. Can store up to 255 characters.
VARCHAR(size)	Holds a variable length string (can contain letters, numbers, and special characters). The maximum size is specified in parenthesis. Can store up to 255 characters. Note: If you put a greater value than 255 it will be converted to a TEXT type
TINYTEXT	Holds a string with a maximum length of 255 characters
TEXT	Holds a string with a maximum length of 65,535 characters
BLOB	For BLOBs (Binary Large OBjects). Holds up to 65,535 bytes of data
MEDIUMTEXT	Holds a string with a maximum length of 16,777,215 characters
MEDIUMBLOB	For BLOBs (Binary Large OBjects). Holds up to 16,777,215 bytes of data
LONGTEXT	Holds a string with a maximum length of 4,294,967,295 characters
LONGBLOB	For BLOBs (Binary Large OBjects). Holds up to 4,294,967,295 bytes of data
ENUM(x,y,z,etc.)	Let you enter a list of possible values. You can list up to 65535 values in an ENUM list. If a value is inserted that is not in the list, a blank value will be inserted. Note: The values are sorted in the order you enter them. You enter the possible values in this format: ENUM('X','Y','Z')
SET	Similar to ENUM except that SET may contain up to 64 list items and can store more than one choice

Integers:

In MySQL, integer data types will have an extra option known as UNSIGNED. Generally, an integer will move to a positive value from a negative one. However, the addition of the UNSIGNED attribute is going to move up that range. As a result, the integer will start at zero and not a negative number.

Data Type (Number)	Description
TINYINT(size)	-128 to 127 normal. 0 to 255 UNSIGNED*. The maximum number of digits may be specified in parenthesis
SMALLINT(size)	-32768 to 32767 normal. 0 to 65535 UNSIGNED*. The maximum number of digits may be specified in parenthesis
MEDIUMINT(size)	-8388608 to 8388607 normal. 0 to 16777215 UNSIGNED*. The maximum number of digits may be specified in parenthesis
INT(size)	-2147483648 to 2147483647 normal. 0 to 4294967295 UNSIGNED*. The maximum number of digits may be specified in parenthesis
BIGINT(size)	-9223372036854775808 to 9223372036854775807 normal. 0 to 18446744073709551615 UNSIGNED*. The maximum number of digits may be specified in parenthesis
FLOAT(size,d)	A small number with a floating decimal point. The maximum number of digits may be specified in the size parameter. The maximum number of digits to the right of the decimal point is specified in the d parameter
DOUBLE(size,d)	A large number with a floating decimal point. The maximum number of digits may be specified in the size parameter. The maximum number of digits to the right of the decimal point is specified in the d parameter
DECIMAL(size,d)	A DOUBLE stored as a string, allowing for a fixed decimal point. The maximum number of digits may be specified in the size parameter. The maximum number of digits to the right of the decimal point is specified in the d parameter

Date/Time:

The two data types, TIMESTAMP and DATETIME may return the same format. However, they work in different ways. TIMESTAMP will set itself automatically to the current time and date in an UPDATE or INSERT query. Different formats are accepted by TIMESTAMP as well.

Data Type (Date)	Description
DATE()	A date. Format: YYYY-MM-DD Note: The supported range is from '1000-01-01' to '9999-12-31'
DATETIME()	*A date and time combination. Format: YYYY-MM-DD HH:MI:SS Note: The supported range is from '1000-01-01 00:00:00' to '9999-12-31 23:59:59'
TIMESTAMP()	*A timestamp. TIMESTAMP values are stored as the number of seconds since the Unix epoch ('1970-01-01 00:00:00' UTC). Format: YYYY-MM-DD HH:MI:SS Note: The supported range is from '1970-01-01 00:00:01' UTC to '2038-01-09 03:14:07' UTC
TIME()	A time. Format: HH:MI:SS Note: The supported range is from '-838:59:59' to '838:59:59'
YEAR()	A year in two-digit or four-digit format. Note: Values allowed in four-digit format: 1901 to 2155. Values allowed in two-digit format: 70 to 69, representing years from 1970 to 2069

Data Types in SQL Server

Like MySQL, the data types in SQL Server can also be classified into different categories. We shall be looking at each one in the following tables.

String:

Data Type (String)	Description	Storage
char(n)	Fixed width character string. Maximum 8,000 characters	Defined width
varchar(n)	Variable width character string. Maximum 8,000 characters	2 bytes + number of chars
varchar(max)	Variable width character string. Maximum 1,073,741,824 characters	2 bytes + number of chars
text	Variable width character string. Maximum 2GB of text data	4 bytes + number of chars
nchar	Fixed width Unicode string. Maximum 4,000 characters	Defined width x 2
nvarchar	Variable width Unicode string. Maximum 4,000 characters	
nvarchar(max)	Variable width Unicode string. Maximum 536,870,912 characters	
ntext	Variable width Unicode string. Maximum 2GB of text data	
bit	Allows 0, 1, or NULL	
binary(n)	Fixed width binary string. Maximum 8,000 bytes	
varbinary	Variable width binary string. Maximum 8,000 bytes	
varbinary(max)	Variable width binary string. Maximum 2GB	
image	Variable width binary string. Maximum 2GB	

Number:

Data Type (Number)	Description	Storage
tinyint	Allows whole numbers from 0 to 255	Stores up to 1 byte
smallint	Allows whole numbers between -32,768 and 32,767	Stores up to 2 bytes
int	Allows whole numbers between -2,147,483,648 and 2,147,483,647	Stores up to 4 bytes
bigint	Allows whole numbers between -9,223,372,036,854,775,808 and 9,223,372,036,854,775,807	Stores up to 8 bytes
decimal(p,s)	Fixed precision and scale numbers. Allows numbers from -10^{38} +1 to 10^{38} −1. The p parameter indicates the maximum total number of digits that can be stored (both to the left and to the right of the decimal point). p must be a value from 1 to 38. Default is 18. The s parameter indicates the maximum number of digits stored to the right of the decimal point. s must be a value from 0 to p. Default value is 0	Stores between 5-17 bytes

numeric(p,s)	Fixed precision and scale numbers. Allows numbers from -$10^{38} + 1$ to $10^{38} - 1$. The p parameter indicates the maximum total number of digits that can be stored (both to the left and to the right of the decimal point). p must be a value from 1 to 38. Default is 18. The s parameter indicates the maximum number of digits stored to the right of the decimal point. s must be a value from 0 to p. Default value is 0	Stores between 5-17 bytes
smallmoney	Monetary data from -214,748.3648 to 214,748.3647	Stores up to 4 bytes
money	Monetary data from -922,337,203,685,477.5808 to 922,337,203,685,477.5807	Stores up to 8 bytes
float(n)	Floating precision number data from -1.79E + 308 to 1.79E + 308. The n parameter indicates whether the field should hold 4 or 8 bytes. float(24) holds a 4-byte field and float(53) holds an 8-byte field. Default value of n is 53.	Stores up to either 4 or 8 bytes depending
real	Floating precision number data from -3.40E + 38 to 3.40E + 38	Stores up to 4 bytes

Date/Time:

Data Type (Date)	Description	Storage
datetime	From January 1, 1753 to December 31, 9999 with an accuracy of 3.33 milliseconds	Stores up to 8 bytes
datetime2	From January 1, 0001 to December 31, 9999 with an accuracy of 100 nanoseconds	Stores between 6-8 bytes
smalldatetime	From January 1, 1900 to June 6, 2079 with an accuracy of 1 minute	Stores up to 4 bytes
date	Store a date only. From January 1, 0001 to December 31, 9999	Stores up to 3 bytes
time	Store a time only to an accuracy of 100 nanoseconds	Stores between 3-5 bytes
datetimeoffset	The same as datetime2 with the addition of a time zone offset	Stores between 8-10 bytes
timestamp	Stores a unique number that gets updated every time a row gets created or modified. The timestamp value is based upon an internal clock and does not correspond to real time. Each table may have only one timestamp variable.	

The above tables will certainly prove to be of immense help in your work. You should certainly go through them more than once to ensure that you have a thorough idea of the data types in use in SQL in different database platforms. In fact, it will be a good idea to mark down the chapter so that you can quickly refer to it whenever you need to refresh your knowledge.

CHAPTER 4

THE BASICS OF FUNCTIONS IN SQL

In any programming language, a function enables you to encapsulate reusable logic to create compostable software. This kind of software is one that has been created from prices which can be reused and assembled in a variety of ways to fulfill the needs of the user. Functions can mask the steps as well as the complexity from the other code.

Be that as it may, functions in SQL have fundamental differences in certain respects from the functions of other programming languages. The fragment of functionality in procedural programming which is known as a function to most programmers will be better referred to as a subroutine. Subroutines are a lot like miniature programs. Subroutines can perform a wide range of actions.

Functions in SQL are more closely related to their mathematical definition. In other words, they map a collection of inputs to a collection of outputs. These functions will accept parameters and perform certain actions to return a result. All of these are made possible without any side effects whatsoever.

On the other hand, they can mask the complexity from the users. They are capable of transforming a complicated chunk of code into something that can be used over and over again. With functions, it becomes possible to create highly complicated search conditions which would be tedious and difficult to express inline.

There are several things you must know about functions in SQL before you can start using them in an effective manner.

Where Can Functions Be Used?

A function, in SQL, can be used nearly in any place where a column or a table can be used. It can also be used in places where a scalar value could be used. It is possible to use functions in constraints or even inside other functions. This versatility is one of the reasons why functions are one of the most powerful features of SQL.

Scalar Functions and Table-Valued Functions

A single value is returned by scalar functions. The type of the value is irrelevant. What matters is that it should be a single value only instead of a table value. A scalar function can be used wherever a scalar expression that has the same data type can be used.

On the other hand, table-valued functions will return a table rather than a single value. Known as TVFs in short, these functions can be used in place where you can use a table. Generally, they are used in the FROM clauses of queries. They are able to encapsulate complicated logic in queries. For example, TVFs can have calculations, business logic and security permissions embedded in them. It becomes easier to create re-usable code frameworks inside the database by using TVFs carefully.

One of the most vital differences between these two types of function is the manner in which they are handled internally.

The majority of developers tend to be work with compliers which inline trivial function calls. This means that the complier is going to incorporate automatically the entire body of the function into its surrounding code in any place where it is called. The alternative to such a procedure is that the function is going to be treated as if it were interpreted code. Invoking a function from the main body of the code will require a jump to another code block for the execution of the function.

Deterministic vs. Nondeterministic

This is another way to classify functions. Understanding this concept is going to be prove helpful in your learning.

Deterministic functions are those which return the same results when called with the same set of parameters as input. For example, a function which adds two numbers will be deterministic as the result is never going to change for those two numbers.

On the other hand, nondeterministic functions may return differing results whenever they are called in spite of the set of inputs remaining the same. The result may also be different even if the data state in the database remains unchanged. One of the best examples of nondeterministic functions is the GETDATE function.

One of the things that you must know about nondeterministic functions is that nearly all of them will be executed once for each statement. They will not be executed for every row.

One of the features of deterministic functions is that they can be used in computed columns and indexed views. However, nondeterministic functions do not have this ability.

Whenever a function is created, the code will be analyzed by the system. It will evaluate if the function is a deterministic or a nondeterministic one. A function which makes a call to any nondeterministic function will also be considered as nondeterministic.

However, to get a proper understanding of the functions available in SQL, we need to take a look at them from a different manner. As such, we shall be looking at Rowset, Aggregate and Ranking functions.

Rowset Functions

These functions will return an object which can be used in a way similar to a view or a table. Every rowset function is a nondeterministic one. In other words, they will be returning a different value whenever they are called even if the set of values remain constant.

Take a look at some of the common rowset functions below.

OPENDATASOURCE:
OPENDATASOURCE (provider_name, init_string).

Example: The following example creates an ad hoc connection to the Payroll instance of SQL Server on server London, and queries the AdventureWorks2012.HumanResources.Employee table. (Use SQLNCLI and SQL Server will redirect to the latest version of SQL Server Native Client OLE DB Provider.)

SELECT *

FROM OPENDATASOURCE('SQLNCLI',

    'Data Source=London\Payroll;Integrated Security=SSPI')

    .AdventureWorks2012.HumanResources.Employee

OPENROWSET:

OPENROWSET

    ({ 'provider_name' , { 'datasource' ; 'user_id' ; 'password'

    | 'provider_string' }

    , { [catalog.] [schema.] object

      | 'query'

    }

    | BULK 'data_file' ,

      { FORMATFILE = 'format_file_path' [<bulk_options>]

      | SINGLE_BLOB | SINGLE_CLOB | SINGLE_NCLOB }

    })

<bulk_options> ::=

[, CODEPAGE = { 'ACP' | 'OEM' | 'RAW' | 'code_page' }]

[, ERRORFILE = 'file_name']

[, FIRSTROW = first_row]

[, LASTROW = last_row]

[, MAXERRORS = maximum_errors]

[, ROWS_PER_BATCH = rows_per_batch]

[, ORDER ({ column [ASC | DESC] } [,...n]) [UNIQUE]

]

Example: The following example uses the SQL Server Native Client OLE DB provider to access the HumanResources.Department table in the AdventureWorks2012 database on the remote server Seattle1. (Use SQLNCLI and SQL Server will redirect to the latest version of SQL Server Native Client OLE DB Provider.) A SELECT statement is used to define the row set returned. The provider string contains the Server and Trusted_Connection keywords. These keywords are recognized by the SQL Server Native Client OLE DB provider.

SELECT a.*

FROM OPENROWSET('SQLNCLI',
'Server=Seattle1;Trusted_Connection=yes;',

'SELECT GroupName, Name, DepartmentID

FROM

AdventureWorks2012.HumanResources.Department

ORDER BY GroupName, Name') AS a;

OPENXML:
OPENXML(idoc int [in] , rowpattern nvarchar [in] , [flags byte [in]])

[WITH (SchemaDeclaration | TableName)]

Example: The following example creates an internal representation of the XML image by using sp_xml_preparedocument. A SELECT statement that uses an OPENXML rowset provider is then executed against the internal representation of the XML document.

The flag value is set to 1. This indicates attribute-centric mapping. Therefore, the XML attributes map to the columns in the rowset. The rowpattern specified as /ROOT/Customer identifies the <Customers> nodes to be processed.

The optional ColPattern (column pattern) parameter is not specified because the column name matches the XML attribute names.

The OPENXML rowset provider creates a two-column rowset (CustomerID and ContactName) from which the SELECT statement retrieves the necessary columns (in this case, all the columns).

DECLARE @idoc int, @doc varchar(1000);

```
SET @doc ='

<ROOT>

<Customer     CustomerID="VINET"     ContactName="Paul
Henriot">

  <Order     CustomerID="VINET"     EmployeeID="5"
OrderDate="1996-07-04T00:00:00">

    <OrderDetail     OrderID="10248"     ProductID="11"
Quantity="12"/>

    <OrderDetail     OrderID="10248"     ProductID="42"
Quantity="10"/>

  </Order>

</Customer>

<Customer     CustomerID="LILAS"     ContactName="Carlos
Gonzlez">

  <Order     CustomerID="LILAS"     EmployeeID="3"
OrderDate="1996-08-16T00:00:00">

    <OrderDetail     OrderID="10283"     ProductID="72"
Quantity="3"/>

  </Order>

</Customer>
```

```
</ROOT>';

--Create an internal representation of the XML document.

EXEC sp_xml_preparedocument @idoc OUTPUT, @doc;

-- Execute a SELECT statement that uses the OPENXML
rowset provider.

SELECT    *

FROM      OPENXML (@idoc, '/ROOT/Customer',1)

          WITH (CustomerID  varchar(10),

          ContactName varchar(20));
```

Resulting in:

```
CustomerID ContactName

---------- --------------------

VINET      Paul Henriot

LILAS      Carlos Gonzlez
```

OPENJSON:

```
OPENJSON( jsonExpression [ , path ] )

    [

        WITH (

            colName type [ column_path ] [ AS JSON ]
```

[, colName type [column_path] [AS JSON]]

[, ... n]

)

]

Example: In this example, list of identifiers are provided as JSON array of numbers. Following query converts JSON array to table of identifiers and filters all products with specified ids.

SET @pSearchOptions = N'[1,2,3,4]'

SELECT * FROM products

INNER JOIN OPENJSON(@pSearchOptions) AS productTypes

ON product.productTypeID = productTypes.value

OPENQUERY:
OPENQUERY (linked_server ,'query')

Example: The following example uses a pass-through UPDATE query against the linked server created in example A.

UPDATE OPENQUERY (OracleSvr, 'SELECT name FROM joe.titles WHERE id = 101')

SET name = 'ADifferentName';   (Microsoft, 2016)

Aggregate Functions

Aggregate functions will perform calculations on a given set of values and a single value will be returned as a result. Null values are ignored by aggregate functions other than COUNT. The aggregate functions are often used in the SELECT statement alongside the GROUP BY clause. These functions are of the deterministic type. In other words, they will be returning the same value whenever they are called with a particular set of values.

Here are some of the aggregate functions that you should know about.

AVG:

AVG ([ALL | DISTINCT] expression)

OVER ([partition_by_clause] order_by_clause)

Example: When used with a GROUP BY clause, each aggregate function produces a single value for each group, instead of for the whole table. The following example produces summary values for each sales territoryin the AdventureWorks2012 database. The summary lists the average bonus received by the sales people in each territory and the sum of year-to-date sales for each territory.

SELECT TerritoryID, AVG(Bonus)as 'Average bonus', SUM(SalesYTD) as 'YTD sales'

FROM Sales.SalesPerson

GROUP BY TerritoryID;

GO

Resulting in:

TerritoryID Average Bonus   YTD Sales

----------- --------------------- ---------------------

NULL   0.00   1252127.9471

1   4133.3333   4502152.2674

2   4100.00   3763178.1787

3   2500.00   3189418.3662

4   2775.00   6709904.1666

5   6700.00   2315185.611

6   2750.00   4058260.1825

7   985.00   3121616.3202

8   75.00   1827066.7118

9   5650.00   1421810.9242

10   5150.00   4116871.2277

(11 row(s) affected)

CHECKSUM_AGG:
CHECKSUM_AGG ([ALL | DISTINCT] expression)

Example: The following example uses CHECKSUM_AGG to detect changes in the Quantity column of the ProductInventory table in the AdventureWorks2012 database.

--Get the checksum value before the column value is changed.

SELECT CHECKSUM_AGG(CAST(Quantity AS int))

FROM Production.ProductInventory;

GO

Resulting in:

287

COUNT:
-- Syntax for SQL Server and Azure SQL Database

COUNT ({ [[ALL | DISTINCT] expression] | * })

[OVER (

[partition_by_clause]

[order_by_clause]

[ROW_or_RANGE_clause]

)]

-- Syntax for Azure SQL Data Warehouse and Parallel Data Warehouse

-- Aggregation Function Syntax

COUNT ({ [[ALL | DISTINCT] expression] | * })

-- Analytic Function Syntax

COUNT ({ expression | * }) OVER ([<partition_by_clause>])

Example: The following example uses the MIN, MAX, AVG and COUNT functions with the OVER clause to provide aggregated values for each department in the HumanResources.Department table in the AdventureWorks2012 database.

SELECT DISTINCT Name

, MIN(Rate) OVER (PARTITION BY edh.DepartmentID) AS MinSalary

, MAX(Rate) OVER (PARTITION BY edh.DepartmentID) AS MaxSalary

, AVG(Rate) OVER (PARTITION BY edh.DepartmentID) AS AvgSalary

,COUNT(edh.BusinessEntityID) OVER (PARTITION BY edh.DepartmentID) AS EmployeesPerDept

FROM HumanResources.EmployeePayHistory AS eph

JOIN HumanResources.EmployeeDepartmentHistory AS edh

ON eph.BusinessEntityID = edh.BusinessEntityID

JOIN HumanResources.Department AS d

ON d.DepartmentID = edh.DepartmentID

WHERE edh.EndDate IS NULL

ORDER BY Name;

Resulting in:

Name	MinSalary	MaxSalary	AvgSalary	EmployeesPerDept
Document Control	10.25	17.7885	14.3884	5
Engineering	32.6923	63.4615	40.1442	6
Executive	39.06	125.50	68.3034	4
Facilities and Maintenance	9.25	24.0385	13.0316	7

Department				
Finance	13.4615	43.2692	23.935	10
Human Resources	13.9423	27.1394	18.0248	6
Information Services	27.4038	50.4808	34.1586	10
Marketing	13.4615	37.50	18.4318	11
Production	6.50	84.1346	13.5537	195
Production Control	8.62	24.5192	16.7746	8
Purchasing	9.86	30.00	18.0202	14
Quality Assurance	10.5769	28.8462	15.4647	6
Research and Development	40.8654	50.4808	43.6731	4
Sales	23.0769	72.1154	29.9719	18

Shipping and Receiving	9.00	19.2308
10.8718	6	
Tool Design	8.62	29.8462
23.5054	6	

(16 row(s) affected)

COUNT_BIG:

-- Syntax for SQL Server and Azure SQL Database

COUNT_BIG ({ [ALL | DISTINCT] expression } | *)

[OVER ([partition_by_clause] [order_by_clause])]

-- Syntax for Azure SQL Data Warehouse and Parallel Data Warehouse

-- Aggregation Function Syntax

COUNT_BIG ({ [[ALL | DISTINCT] expression] | * })

-- Analytic Function Syntax

COUNT_BIG ({ expression | * }) OVER ([<partition_by_clause>])

Example: See previous example.

GROUPING:

GROUPING (<column_expression>)

Example: The following example groups SalesQuota and aggregates SaleYTD amounts in the AdventureWorks2012 database. The GROUPING function is applied to the SalesQuota column.

SELECT SalesQuota, SUM(SalesYTD) 'TotalSalesYTD', GROUPING(SalesQuota) AS 'Grouping'

FROM Sales.SalesPerson

GROUP BY SalesQuota WITH ROLLUP;

GO

Resulting in:

SalesQuota TotalSalesYTD Grouping

------------ ------------------ --------

NULL 1533087.5999 0

250000.00 33461260.59 0

300000.00 9299677.9445 0

NULL 44294026.1344 1

(4 row(s) affected)

GROUPING_JD:
GROUPING_ID (<column_expression>[,...n])

Example: In this example, the GROUPING_ID() function is used to create a value for each row in the Grouping Level column to identify the level of grouping.

Unlike ROLLUP in the previous example, CUBE outputs all grouping levels. If the order of the columns in the CUBE list is changed, the level values in the Grouping Level column will also have to be changed. The example uses the AdventureWorks2012 database

SELECT DATEPART(yyyy,OrderDate) AS N'Year'

,DATEPART(mm,OrderDate) AS N'Month'

,DATEPART(dd,OrderDate) AS N'Day'

,SUM(TotalDue) AS N'Total Due'

,CAST(GROUPING(DATEPART(dd,OrderDate))AS char(1)) +

CAST(GROUPING(DATEPART(mm,OrderDate))AS char(1)) +

CAST(GROUPING(DATEPART(yyyy,OrderDate))AS char(1))

AS N'Bit Vector(base-2)'

,GROUPING_ID(DATEPART(yyyy,OrderDate)

,DATEPART(mm,OrderDate)

```
    ,DATEPART(dd,OrderDate))

    AS N'Integer Equivalent'

,CASE

    WHEN GROUPING_ID(DATEPART(yyyy,OrderDate)

,DATEPART(mm,OrderDate),DATEPART(dd,OrderDate)

    ) = 0 THEN N'Year Month Day'

    WHEN GROUPING_ID(DATEPART(yyyy,OrderDate)

,DATEPART(mm,OrderDate),DATEPART(dd,OrderDate)

    ) = 1 THEN N'Year Month'

    WHEN GROUPING_ID(DATEPART(yyyy,OrderDate)

,DATEPART(mm,OrderDate),DATEPART(dd,OrderDate)

    ) = 2 THEN N'Year Day'

    WHEN GROUPING_ID(DATEPART(yyyy,OrderDate)

,DATEPART(mm,OrderDate),DATEPART(dd,OrderDate)

    ) = 3 THEN N'Year'
```

```sql
        WHEN GROUPING_ID(DATEPART(yyyy,OrderDate)

,DATEPART(mm,OrderDate),DATEPART(dd,OrderDate)

        ) = 4 THEN N'Month Day'

        WHEN GROUPING_ID(DATEPART(yyyy,OrderDate)

,DATEPART(mm,OrderDate),DATEPART(dd,OrderDate)

        ) = 5 THEN N'Month'

        WHEN GROUPING_ID(DATEPART(yyyy,OrderDate)

,DATEPART(mm,OrderDate),DATEPART(dd,OrderDate)

        ) = 6 THEN N'Day'

        WHEN GROUPING_ID(DATEPART(yyyy,OrderDate)

,DATEPART(mm,OrderDate),DATEPART(dd,OrderDate)

        ) = 7 THEN N'Grand Total'

    ELSE N'Error'

    END AS N'Grouping Level'

    FROM Sales.SalesOrderHeader
```

WHERE DATEPART(yyyy,OrderDate) IN(N'2007',N'2008')

AND DATEPART(mm,OrderDate) IN(1,2)

AND DATEPART(dd,OrderDate) IN(1,2)

GROUP BY CUBE(DATEPART(yyyy,OrderDate)

,DATEPART(mm,OrderDate)

,DATEPART(dd,OrderDate))

ORDER BY GROUPING_ID(DATEPART(yyyy,OrderDate)

,DATEPART(mm,OrderDate)

,DATEPART(dd,OrderDate)

)

,DATEPART(yyyy,OrderDate)

,DATEPART(mm,OrderDate)

,DATEPART(dd,OrderDate);

Resulting in (partial results):

2007   1   1   1497452.6066 000   0   Year
Month Day

2007   1   2   21772.3494   000   0   Year
Month Day

2007	2	1	2705653.5913	000	0	Year Month Day
2007	2	2	21684.4068	000	0	Year Month Day
2008	1	1	1908122.0967	000	0	Year Month Day
2008	1	2	46458.0691	000	0	Year Month Day
2008	2	1	3108771.9729	000	0	Year Month Day
2008	2	2	54598.5488	000	0	Year Month Day
2007	1	NULL	1519224.956	100	1	Year Month
2007	2	NULL	2727337.9981	100	1	Year Month
2008	1	NULL	1954580.1658	100	1	Year Month
2008	2	NULL	3163370.5217	100	1	Year Month
2007	NULL	1	4203106.1979	010	2	Year Day

2007	NULL	2	43456.7562	010	2	Year Day
2008	NULL	1	5016894.0696	010	2	Year Day
2008	NULL	2	101056.6179	010	2	Year Day
2007	NULL	NULL	4246562.9541	110	3	Year
2008	NULL	NULL	5117950.6875	110	3	Year
NULL	1	1	3405574.7033	001	4	Month Day
NULL	1	2	68230.4185	001	4	Month Day
NULL	2	1	5814425.5642	001	4	Month Day
NULL	2	2	76282.9556	001	4	Month Day
NULL	1	NULL	3473805.1218	101	5	Month
NULL	2	NULL	5890708.5198	101	5	Month
NULL	NULL	1	9220000.2675	011	6	Day
NULL	NULL	2	144513.3741	011	6	Day
NULL	NULL	NULL	9364513.6416	111	7	Grand Total

MAX:

-- Syntax for SQL Server and Azure SQL Database

MAX ([ALL | DISTINCT] expression)

OVER ([partition_by_clause] order_by_clause)

-- Syntax for Azure SQL Data Warehouse and Parallel Data Warehouse

-- Aggregation Function Syntax

MAX ([ALL | DISTINCT] expression)

-- Aggregation Function Syntax

MAX (expression) OVER ([<partition_by_clause>] [<order_by_clause>])

Example: The following example uses the MIN, MAX, AVG and COUNT functions with the OVER clause to provide aggregated values for each department in the HumanResources.Department table in the AdventureWorks2012 database.

SELECT DISTINCT Name

, MIN(Rate) OVER (PARTITION BY edh.DepartmentID) AS MinSalary

, MAX(Rate) OVER (PARTITION BY edh.DepartmentID) AS MaxSalary

```sql
, AVG(Rate) OVER (PARTITION BY edh.DepartmentID)
AS AvgSalary

,COUNT(edh.BusinessEntityID) OVER (PARTITION BY
edh.DepartmentID) AS EmployeesPerDept

FROM HumanResources.EmployeePayHistory AS eph

JOIN HumanResources.EmployeeDepartmentHistory AS edh

ON eph.BusinessEntityID = edh.BusinessEntityID

JOIN HumanResources.Department AS d

ON d.DepartmentID = edh.DepartmentID

WHERE edh.EndDate IS NULL

ORDER BY Name;
```

Resulting in:

Name	MinSalary	MaxSalary	AvgSalary	EmployeesPerDept
Document Control	10.25	17.7885	14.3884	5
Engineering	32.6923	63.4615	40.1442	6

Department				
Executive	39.06	125.50	68.3034	4
Facilities and Maintenance	9.25	24.0385	13.0316	7
Finance	13.4615	43.2692	23.935	10
Human Resources	13.9423	27.1394	18.0248	6
Information Services	27.4038	50.4808	34.1586	10
Marketing	13.4615	37.50	18.4318	11
Production	6.50	84.1346	13.5537	195
Production Control	8.62	24.5192	16.7746	8
Purchasing	9.86	30.00	18.0202	14
Quality Assurance	10.5769	28.8462	15.4647	6

Research and Development	40.8654	50.4808
43.6731 4		
Sales	23.0769	72.1154
29.9719 18		
Shipping and Receiving	9.00	19.2308
10.8718 6		
Tool Design	8.62	29.8462
23.5054 6		

(16 row(s) affected)

MIN:

-- Syntax for SQL Server and Azure SQL Database

MIN ([ALL | DISTINCT] expression)

OVER ([partition_by_clause] order_by_clause)

-- Syntax for Azure SQL Data Warehouse and Parallel Data Warehouse

-- Aggregation Function Syntax

MIN ([ALL | DISTINCT] expression)

-- Aggregation Function Syntax

MIN (expression) OVER ([<partition_by_clause>] [<order_by_clause>])

Example: The following example uses the MIN, MAX, AVG and COUNT functions with the OVER clause to provide aggregated values for each department in the Human Resources. Department table in the AdventureWorks2012 database.

```
SELECT DISTINCT Name

    , MIN(Rate) OVER (PARTITION BY edh.DepartmentID)
AS MinSalary

    ,    MAX(Rate)    OVER    (PARTITION    BY
edh.DepartmentID) AS MaxSalary

    , AVG(Rate) OVER (PARTITION BY edh.DepartmentID)
AS AvgSalary

    ,COUNT(edh.BusinessEntityID) OVER (PARTITION BY
edh.DepartmentID) AS EmployeesPerDept

FROM HumanResources.EmployeePayHistory AS eph

JOIN HumanResources.EmployeeDepartmentHistory AS edh

ON eph.BusinessEntityID = edh.BusinessEntityID

JOIN HumanResources.Department AS d

ON d.DepartmentID = edh.DepartmentID

WHERE edh.EndDate IS NULL

ORDER BY Name;
```

Resulting in:

Name	MinSalary	MaxSalary	AvgSalary	EmployeesPerDept
Document Control	10.25	17.7885	14.3884	5
Engineering	32.6923	63.4615	40.1442	6
Executive	39.06	125.50	68.3034	4
Facilities and Maintenance	9.25	24.0385	13.0316	7
Finance	13.4615	43.2692	23.935	10
Human Resources	13.9423	27.1394	18.0248	6
Information Services	27.4038	50.4808	34.1586	10
Marketing	13.4615	37.50	18.4318	11

Production	6.50	84.1346	13.5537	195
Production Control	8.62	24.5192	16.7746	8
Purchasing	9.86	30.00	18.0202	14
Quality Assurance	10.5769	28.8462	15.4647	6
Research and Development	40.8654	50.4808	43.6731	4
Sales	23.0769	72.1154	29.9719	18
Shipping and Receiving	9.00	19.2308	10.8718	6
Tool Design	8.62	29.8462	23.5054	6

(16 row(s) affected)

SUM:

-- Syntax for SQL Server and Azure SQL Database

SUM ([ALL | DISTINCT] expression)

OVER ([partition_by_clause] order_by_clause)

-- Syntax for Azure SQL Data Warehouse and Parallel Data Warehouse

SUM ([ALL | DISTINCT] expression)

Example: The following example uses the SUM function with the OVER clause to provide a cumulative total of yearly sales for each territory in the Sales.SalesPerson table in the AdventureWorks2012 database. The data is partitioned by TerritoryID and logically ordered by SalesYTD. This means that the SUM function is computed for each territory based on the sales year. Notice that for TerritoryID 1, there are two rows for sales year 2005 representing the two sales people with sales that year. The cumulative sales for these two rows is computed and then the third row representing sales for the year 2006 is included in the computation.

SELECT BusinessEntityID, TerritoryID

,DATEPART(yy,ModifiedDate) AS SalesYear

,CONVERT(varchar(20),SalesYTD,1) AS SalesYTD

,CONVERT(varchar(20),AVG(SalesYTD)   OVER (PARTITION BY TerritoryID

                          ORDER   BY DATEPART(yy,ModifiedDate)

                          ),1) AS MovingAvg

```
              ,CONVERT(varchar(20),SUM(SalesYTD)          OVER
(PARTITION BY TerritoryID

                              ORDER                        BY
DATEPART(yy,ModifiedDate)

                              ),1) AS CumulativeTotal

    FROM Sales.SalesPerson

    WHERE TerritoryID IS NULL OR TerritoryID < 5

    ORDER BY TerritoryID,SalesYear;
```

BusinessEntityID	TerritoryID	SalesYear	SalesYTD	MovingAvg	CumulativeTotal
274	NULL	2005	559,697.56	559,697.56	559,697.56
287	NULL	2006	519,905.93	539,801.75	1,079,603.50
285	NULL	2007	172,524.45	417,375.98	1,252,127.95
283	1	2005	1,573,012.94	1,462,795.04	2,925,590.07

280	1	2005	1,352,577.13	1,462,795.04
2,925,590.07				
284	1	2006	1,576,562.20	1,500,717.42
4,502,152.27				
275	2	2005	3,763,178.18	3,763,178.18
3,763,178.18				
277	3	2005	3,189,418.37	3,189,418.37
3,189,418.37				
276	4	2005	4,251,368.55	3,354,952.08
6,709,904.17				
281	4	2005	2,458,535.62	3,354,952.08
6,709,904.17				

(10 row(s) affected)

2nd example:

In this example, the OVER clause does not include PARTITION BY. This means that the function will be applied to all rows returned by the query. The ORDER BY clause specified in the OVER clause determines the logical order to which the SUM function is applied. The query returns a cumulative total of sales by year for all sales territories specified in the WHERE clause. The ORDER BY clause specified in the SELECT statement determines the order in which the rows of the query are displayed.

```sql
SELECT BusinessEntityID, TerritoryID

,DATEPART(yy,ModifiedDate) AS SalesYear

,CONVERT(varchar(20),SalesYTD,1) AS  SalesYTD

,CONVERT(varchar(20),AVG(SalesYTD)  OVER  (ORDER
BY DATEPART(yy,ModifiedDate)

                       ),1) AS MovingAvg

,CONVERT(varchar(20),SUM(SalesYTD)  OVER  (ORDER
BY DATEPART(yy,ModifiedDate)

                       ),1) AS CumulativeTotal

FROM Sales.SalesPerson

WHERE TerritoryID IS NULL OR TerritoryID < 5

ORDER BY SalesYear;
```

Resulting in:

BusinessEntityID	TerritoryID	SalesYear	SalesYTD	MovingAvg	CumulativeTotal
274	NULL	2005	559,697.56	2,449,684.05	17,147,788.35

275	2	2005	3,763,178.18	2,449,684.05	17,147,788.35
276	4	2005	4,251,368.55	2,449,684.05	17,147,788.35
277	3	2005	3,189,418.37	2,449,684.05	17,147,788.35
280	1	2005	1,352,577.13	2,449,684.05	17,147,788.35
281	4	2005	2,458,535.62	2,449,684.05	17,147,788.35
283	1	2005	1,573,012.94	2,449,684.05	17,147,788.35
284	1	2006	1,576,562.20	2,138,250.72	19,244,256.47
287	NULL	2006	519,905.93	2,138,250.72	19,244,256.47
285	NULL	2007	172,524.45	1,941,678.09	19,416,780.93

(10 row(s) affected)

STDEV:

-- Syntax for SQL Server and Azure SQL Database

STDEV ([ALL | DISTINCT] expression)

OVER ([partition_by_clause] order_by_clause)

-- Syntax for Azure SQL Data Warehouse and Parallel Data Warehouse

-- Aggregate Function Syntax

STDEV ([ALL | DISTINCT] expression)

-- Analytic Function Syntax

STDEV (expression) OVER ([partition_by_clause] order_by_clause)

Example: The following example returns the standard deviation for all bonus values in the SalesPerson table in the AdventureWorks2012 database.

SELECT STDEV(Bonus)

FROM Sales.SalesPerson;

GO

STDEVP:

-- Syntax for SQL Server and Azure SQL Database

STDEVP ([ALL | DISTINCT] expression)

OVER ([partition_by_clause] order_by_clause)

-- Syntax for Azure SQL Data Warehouse and Parallel Data Warehouse

-- Aggregate Function Syntax

STDEVP ([ALL | DISTINCT] expression)

-- Analytic Function Syntax

STDEVP (expression) OVER ([partition_by_clause] order_by_clause)

Example: The following example returns the STDEVP of the sales quota values in the table dbo.FactSalesQuota. The first column contains the standard deviation of all distinct values and the second column contains the standard deviation of all values including any duplicates values.

-- Uses AdventureWorks

SELECT STDEVP(DISTINCT SalesAmountQuota)AS Distinct_Values, STDEVP(SalesAmountQuota) AS All_Values

FROM dbo.FactSalesQuota;SELECT STDEVP(DISTINCT Quantity)AS Distinct_Values, STDEVP(Quantity) AS All_Values

FROM ProductInventory;

VAR:
-- Syntax for SQL Server and Azure SQL Database

VAR ([ALL | DISTINCT] expression)

OVER ([partition_by_clause] order_by_clause)

-- Syntax for Azure SQL Data Warehouse and Parallel Data Warehouse

-- Aggregate Function Syntax

VAR ([ALL | DISTINCT] expression)

-- Analytic Function Syntax

VAR (expression) OVER ([partition_by_clause] order_by_clause)

Example: The following example returns the variance for all bonus values in the SalesPerson table in the AdventureWorks2012 database.

SELECT VAR(Bonus)

FROM Sales.SalesPerson;

GO

VARP:
-- Syntax for SQL Server and Azure SQL Database

VARP ([ALL | DISTINCT] expression)

OVER ([partition_by_clause] order_by_clause) nh

-- Syntax for Azure SQL Data Warehouse and Parallel Data Warehouse

-- Aggregate Function Syntax

VARP ([ALL | DISTINCT] expression)

-- Analytic Function Syntax

VARP (expression) OVER ([partition_by_clause] order_by_clause)

Example: The following example returns the variance for the population for all bonus values in the SalesPerson table in the AdventureWorks2012 database.

SELECT VARP(Bonus)

FROM Sales.SalesPerson;

GO

(Microsoft, 2010)

Ranking Functions

A ranking value will be returned by ranking functions for each and every row present in a partition. A rank of some kind will, thereby, be associated with the rows. It is possible for some rows to receive the exact value which other rows already have depending on which function has been used. Ranking functions are of the nondeterministic variety.

Check out some ranking functions in the following list.

RANK:

-- Syntax for SQL Server, Azure SQL Database, Azure SQL Data Warehouse, Parallel Data Warehouse

RANK ( ) OVER ([partition_by_clause] order_by_clause)

Example: The following example ranks the products in inventory the specified inventory locations according to their quantities. The result set is partitioned by LocationID and logically ordered by Quantity. Notice that products 494 and 495 have the same quantity. Because they are tied, they are both ranked one.

USE AdventureWorks2012;

GO

SELECT i.ProductID, p.Name, i.LocationID, i.Quantity

,RANK() OVER

(PARTITION BY i.LocationID ORDER BY i.Quantity DESC) AS Rank

FROM Production.ProductInventory AS i

INNER JOIN Production.Product AS p

ON i.ProductID = p.ProductID

WHERE i.LocationID BETWEEN 3 AND 4

ORDER BY i.LocationID;

GO

Results in:

ProductID	Name	LocationID	Quantity	Rank
494	Paint - Silver	3	49	1
495	Paint - Blue	3	49	1
493	Paint - Red	3	41	3
496	Paint - Yellow	3	30	4
492	Paint - Black	3	17	5
495	Paint - Blue	4	35	1
496	Paint - Yellow	4	25	2
493	Paint - Red	4	24	3
492	Paint - Black	4	14	4
494	Paint - Silver	4	12	5

(10 row(s) affected)

NTILE:

-- Syntax for SQL Server, Azure SQL Database, Azure SQL Data Warehouse, Parallel Data Warehouse

NTILE (integer_expression) OVER ([<partition_by_clause>] < order_by_clause >)

Example: The following example divides rows into four groups of employees based on their year-to-date sales. Because the total number of rows is not divisible by the number of groups, the first two groups have four rows and the remaining groups have three rows each.

USE AdventureWorks2012;

GO

SELECT p.FirstName, p.LastName

,NTILE(4) OVER(ORDER BY SalesYTD DESC) AS Quartile

,CONVERT(nvarchar(20),s.SalesYTD,1) AS SalesYTD

, a.PostalCode

FROM Sales.SalesPerson AS s

INNER JOIN Person.Person AS p

ON s.BusinessEntityID = p.BusinessEntityID

INNER JOIN Person.Address AS a

ON a.AddressID = p.BusinessEntityID

WHERE TerritoryID IS NOT NULL

```
        AND SalesYTD <> 0;

        GO

        Results in:

        FirstName      LastName                    Quartile  SalesYTD
PostalCode

        -------------  --------------------- --------- -------------- ----------

        Linda          Mitchell                  1       4,251,368.55
98027

        Jae            Pak                       1       4,116,871.23
98055

        Michael        Blythe                    1       3,763,178.18
98027

        Jillian        Carson                    1       3,189,418.37
98027

        Ranjit         Varkey Chudukatil         2       3,121,616.32
98055

        José           Saraiva                   2       2,604,540.72
98055

        Shu            Ito                       2       2,458,535.62
98055
```

Tsvi	Reiter	2	2,315,185.61
98027			
Rachel	Valdez	3	1,827,066.71
98055			
Tete	Mensa-Annan	3	1,576,562.20
98055			
David	Campbell	3	1,573,012.94
98055			
Garrett	Vargas	4	1,453,719.47
98027			
Lynn	Tsoflias	4	1,421,810.92 98055
Pamela	Ansman-Wolfe	4	1,352,577.13 98027

(14 row(s) affected)

DENSE_RANK:

- Syntax for SQL Server, Azure SQL Database, Azure SQL Data Warehouse, Parallel Data Warehouse

    DENSE_RANK ( ) OVER ([<partition_by_clause>] < order_by_clause >)

Example: The following example ranks the products in inventory the specified inventory locations according to their quantities. The result set is partitioned by LocationID and logically ordered by Quantity. Notice that products 494 and 495 have the same quantity. Because they are tied, they are both ranked one.

```
USE AdventureWorks2012;

GO

SELECT i.ProductID, p.Name, i.LocationID, i.Quantity

    ,DENSE_RANK() OVER

    (PARTITION BY i.LocationID ORDER BY i.Quantity DESC) AS Rank

FROM Production.ProductInventory AS i

INNER JOIN Production.Product AS p

    ON i.ProductID = p.ProductID

WHERE i.LocationID BETWEEN 3 AND 4

ORDER BY i.LocationID;

GO
```

Results in:

ProductID	Name	LocationID	Quantity	Rank
494	Paint - Silver	3	49	1

495	Paint - Blue	3	49	1
493	Paint - Red	3	41	2
496	Paint - Yellow	3	30	3
492	Paint - Black	3	17	4
495	Paint - Blue	4	35	1
496	Paint - Yellow	4	25	2
493	Paint - Red	4	24	3
492	Paint - Black	4	14	4
494	Paint - Silver	4	12	5

(10 row(s) affected)

ROW_NUMBER:

-- Syntax for SQL Server, Azure SQL Database, Azure SQL Data Warehouse, Parallel Data Warehouse

ROW_NUMBER ( )

OVER ([PARTITION BY value_expression , ... [n]] order_by_clause)

Example: The following example calculates a row number for the salespeople in Adventure Works Cycles based on their year-to-date sales ranking.

USE AdventureWorks2012;

GO

```
SELECT ROW_NUMBER() OVER(ORDER BY SalesYTD
DESC) AS Row,
    FirstName, LastName, ROUND(SalesYTD,2,1) AS "Sales
YTD"
FROM Sales.vSalesPerson
WHERE TerritoryName IS NOT NULL AND SalesYTD <> 0;
```

Results in:

```
Row    FirstName    LastName
SalesYTD

--- -----------  ---------------------- -----------------

1      Linda        Mitchell
4251368.54

2      Jae          Pak
4116871.22

3      Michael      Blythe
3763178.17

4      Jillian      Carson
3189418.36
```

5   Ranjit   Varkey   Chudukatil
3121616.32

6   José   Saraiva
2604540.71

7   Shu   Ito
2458535.61

8   Tsvi   Reiter
2315185.61

9   Rachel   Valdez
1827066.71

10   Tete   Mensa-Annan
1576562.19

11   David   Campbell
1573012.93

12   Garrett   Vargas
1453719.46

13   Lynn   Tsoflias
1421810.92

14   Pamela   Ansman-Wolfe   1352577.13

The above list should have given you a good idea of how those functions work. Go through the examples of each function and the results they return. Understand how they work so that you can start using them as well.

CHAPTER 5

GUIDE TO SCALAR FUNCTIONS

Scalar functions are one of the most important groups of functions

you will encounter in SQL. As such, it becomes important to tackle them separately. We shall be taking a comprehensive look in this chapter into the various scalar functions you will be using in SQL. Before we do so, let us first understand what scalar functions are.

What Are Scalar Functions?

A scalar function operates exclusively on scalar values. In other words, it will take input value as the argument directly and then return a single value. Sounds familiar? Well, it does share certain points of similarity with aggregate functions. However, there is a major difference between them. Scalar functions will operate with just a single value and only a single value will be returned. These functions will not return a table.

Moreover, it is possible to place scalar functions anywhere. A scalar function is capable of using all scalar data types expect user-defined data and TIMESTAMP.

Let us now take a look at the various kinds of scalar functions that you will be using in SQL.

@@DATEFIRST:

-- Syntax for SQL Server, Azure SQL Database, Azure SQL Data Warehouse, Parallel Data Warehouse

@@DATEFIRST

Example: The following example sets the first day of the week to 5 (Friday), and assumes the current day, Today, to be Saturday. The SELECT statement returns the DATEFIRST value and the number of the current day of the week.

SET DATEFIRST 5;

SELECT @@DATEFIRST AS 'First Day'

,DATEPART(dw, SYSDATETIME()) AS 'Today';

Results in:

First Day   Today

---------------- --------------

5   2

@@DBTS:

Example: The following example returns the current timestamp from the AdventureWorks2012 database.

USE AdventureWorks2012;

GO

SELECT @@DBTS;

@@LANGID:

Example: The following example sets the language for the current session to Italian, and then uses @@LANGID to return the ID for Italian.

SET LANGUAGE 'Italian'

SELECT @@LANGID AS 'Language ID'

Results in:

Changed language setting to Italiano.

Language ID

6

@@LANGUAGE:
-- Syntax for SQL Server, Azure SQL Database, Azure SQL Data Warehouse, Parallel Data Warehouse

@@LANGUAGE

Example: The following example returns the language for the current session.

SELECT @@LANGUAGE AS 'Language Name';

Resulting in:

Language Name

----

us_english

@@LOCK_TIMEOUT:
@@LOCK_TIMEOUT

Example: This example shows the result set when a LOCK_TIMEOUT value is not set.

```
SELECT @@LOCK_TIMEOUT AS [Lock Timeout];

GO
```

Resulting in:

Lock Timeout

-1

@@MAX_CONNECTIONS:
Example: The following example shows returning the maximum number of user connections on an instance of SQL Server. The example assumes that SQL Server has not been reconfigured for fewer user connections.

```
SELECT @@MAX_CONNECTIONS AS 'Max Connections';
```

Resulting in:

Max Connections

32767

@@MAX_PRECISION:
Example: SELECT @@MAX_PRECISION AS 'Max Precision'

@@NESTLEVEL:
@@NESTLEVEL

Example: The following example creates two procedures: one that calls the other, and one that displays the @@NESTLEVEL setting of each.

```
USE AdventureWorks2012;

GO

IF OBJECT_ID (N'usp_OuterProc', N'P')IS NOT NULL

    DROP PROCEDURE usp_OuterProc;

GO

IF OBJECT_ID (N'usp_InnerProc', N'P')IS NOT NULL

    DROP PROCEDURE usp_InnerProc;

GO

CREATE PROCEDURE usp_InnerProc AS
```

```
    SELECT @@NESTLEVEL AS 'Inner Level';

GO

CREATE PROCEDURE usp_OuterProc AS

    SELECT @@NESTLEVEL AS 'Outer Level';

    EXEC usp_InnerProc;

GO

EXECUTE usp_OuterProc;

GO
```

Results in:

```
Outer Level

-----------

1

Inner Level

-----------

2
```

@@OPTIONS:

Example: The following example demonstrates the difference in concatenation behavior with two different setting of the CONCAT_NULL_YIELDS_NULL option.

SELECT @@OPTIONS AS OriginalOptionsValue;

SET CONCAT_NULL_YIELDS_NULL OFF;

SELECT 'abc' + NULL AS ResultWhen_OFF, @@OPTIONS AS OptionsValueWhen_OFF;

SET CONCAT_NULL_YIELDS_NULL ON;

SELECT 'abc' + NULL AS ResultWhen_ON, @@OPTIONS AS OptionsValueWhen_ON;

@@REMSERVER:

Example: The following example creates the procedure usp_CheckServer that returns the name of the remote server

CREATE PROCEDURE usp_CheckServer

AS

SELECT @@REMSERVER;

The following stored procedure is created on the local server SEATTLE1. The user logs on to a remote server, LONDON2, and runs usp_CheckServer.

Results in:

Server Name

ACCTG

EXEC SEATTLE1...usp_CheckServer;

\-\-\-\-\-\-\-\-\-\-\-\-\-\-\-

LONDON2

@@SERVERNAME:

Example: SELECT @@SERVERNAME AS 'Server Name'

@@SERVICENAME:

Example: SELECT @@SERVICENAME AS 'Service Name';

Resulting in:

Service Name

\-

MSSQLSERVER

@@SPID:

-- Syntax for SQL Server, Azure SQL Database, Azure SQL Data Warehouse, Parallel Data Warehouse

@@SPID
Example: SELECT @@SPID AS 'ID', SYSTEM_USER AS 'Login Name', USER AS 'User Name';

Results in:

ID   Login Name   User Name

\-\-\-\-\-\- \- \-

@@TEXTSIZE:

Example: -- Set the TEXTSIZE option to the default size of 4096 bytes.

SET TEXTSIZE 0

SELECT @@TEXTSIZE AS 'Text Size'

SET TEXTSIZE 2048

SELECT @@TEXTSIZE AS 'Text Size'

Resulting in:

Text Size

4096

Text Size

2048

@@VERSION:

-- Syntax for SQL Server, Azure SQL Database, Azure SQL Data Warehouse, Parallel Data Warehouse

@@VERSION

Example: SELECT @@VERSION AS 'SQL Server Version';

CAST and CONVERT:

-- Syntax for SQL Server, Azure SQL Database, Azure SQL Data Warehouse, Parallel Data Warehouse

-- Syntax for CAST:

CAST (expression AS data_type [(length)])

-- Syntax for CONVERT:

CONVERT (data_type [(length)] , expression [, style])

Example: Each example retrieves the name of the product for those products that have a 3 in the first digit of their list price and converts their ListPrice to int.

-- Use CAST

USE AdventureWorks2012;

GO

SELECT SUBSTRING(Name, 1, 30) AS ProductName, ListPrice

FROM Production.Product

WHERE CAST(ListPrice AS int) LIKE '3%';

GO

-- Use CONVERT.

USE AdventureWorks2012;

GO

SELECT SUBSTRING(Name, 1, 30) AS ProductName, ListPrice

FROM Production.Product

WHERE CONVERT(int, ListPrice) LIKE '3%';

GO

The following example calculates a single column computation (Computed) by dividing the total year-to-date sales (SalesYTD) by the commission percentage (CommissionPCT). This result is converted to an int data type after being rounded to the nearest whole number.

USE AdventureWorks2012;

GO

SELECT CAST(ROUND(SalesYTD/CommissionPCT, 0) AS int) AS Computed

FROM Sales.SalesPerson

WHERE CommissionPCT != 0;

GO

Resulting in:

Computed

379753754

346698349

257144242

176493899

281101272

0

301872549

212623750

298948202

250784119

239246890

101664220

124511336

97688107

(14 row(s) affected)

PARSE:

PARSE (string_value AS data_type [USING culture])

Example: SELECT PARSE('Monday, 13 December 2010' AS datetime2 USING 'en-US') AS Result;

Resulting in:

Result

2010-12-13 00:00:00.0000000

(1 row(s) affected)

TRY_CAST:

TRY_CAST (expression AS data_type [(length)])

Example: The following example demonstrates that TRY_CAST returns null when the cast fails.

SELECT

CASE WHEN TRY_CAST('test' AS float) IS NULL

THEN 'Cast failed'

ELSE 'Cast succeeded'

END AS Result;

GO

Results in:

Result

Cast failed

(1 row(s) affected)

TRY_CONVERT:

TRY_CONVERT (data_type [(length)], expression [, style])

Example:

SELECT

    CASE WHEN TRY_CONVERT(float, 'test') IS NULL

    THEN 'Cast failed'

    ELSE 'Cast succeeded'

END AS Result;

GO

Results in:

Result

Cast failed

(1 row(s) affected)

TRY_PARSE:

TRY_PARSE (string_value AS data_type [USING culture])

Example: SELECT TRY_PARSE('Jabberwokkie' AS datetime2 USING 'en-US') AS Result;

Resulting in:

Result

NULL

(1 row(s) affected)

@@CURSOR_ROWS:

Example: The following example declares a cursor and uses SELECT to display the value of @@CURSOR_ROWS. The setting has a value of 0 before the cursor is opened and a value of -1 to indicate that the cursor keyset is populated asynchronously.

USE AdventureWorks2012;

GO

SELECT @@CURSOR_ROWS;

DECLARE Name_Cursor CURSOR FOR

SELECT   LastName   ,@@CURSOR_ROWS   FROM Person.Person;

OPEN Name_Cursor;

FETCH NEXT FROM Name_Cursor;

SELECT @@CURSOR_ROWS;

CLOSE Name_Cursor;

DEALLOCATE Name_Cursor;

GO

Resulting in:

0

LastName

Sanchez

-1

@@FETCH_STATUS:

Example: The following example uses @@FETCH_STATUS to control cursor activities in a WHILE loop.

```
DECLARE Employee_Cursor CURSOR FOR

SELECT BusinessEntityID, JobTitle

FROM AdventureWorks2012.HumanResources.Employee;

OPEN Employee_Cursor;

FETCH NEXT FROM Employee_Cursor;

WHILE @@FETCH_STATUS = 0

   BEGIN

      FETCH NEXT FROM Employee_Cursor;

   END;

CLOSE Employee_Cursor;

DEALLOCATE Employee_Cursor;

GO
```

CURSOR_STATUS:
CURSOR_STATUS

```
        (

             { 'local' , 'cursor_name' }

             | { 'global' , 'cursor_name' }

             | { 'variable' , 'cursor_variable' }
```

)

Example: The following example uses the CURSOR_STATUS function to show the status of a cursor before and after it is opened and closed.

```
CREATE TABLE #TMP

(

  ii int

)

GO

INSERT INTO #TMP(ii) VALUES(1)

INSERT INTO #TMP(ii) VALUES(2)

INSERT INTO #TMP(ii) VALUES(3)

GO

--Create a cursor.

DECLARE cur CURSOR

FOR SELECT * FROM #TMP

--Display the status of the cursor before and after opening

--closing the cursor.

SELECT CURSOR_STATUS('global','cur') AS 'After declare'
```

OPEN cur

SELECT CURSOR_STATUS('global','cur') AS 'After Open'

CLOSE cur

SELECT CURSOR_STATUS('global','cur') AS 'After Close'

--Remove the cursor.

DEALLOCATE cur

--Drop the table.

DROP TABLE #TMP

Resulting in:

After declare

-1

After Open

1

After Close

-1

ISJSON: (Microsoft, 2016)

ISJSON (expression)

Example: The following example runs a statement block conditionally if the parameter value contains valid JSON.

IF (ISJSON(@param) > 0)

BEGIN

    -- Do something with the valid JSON value of @param.

END

JSON_VALUE:

JSON_VALUE (expression , path)

Example: The following example uses the values of JSON properties in query results. Since JSON_VALUE preserves the collation of the source, the sort order of the results depends on the collation of the jsonInfo column

SELECT FirstName, LastName,

    JSON_VALUE(jsonInfo, '$.info.address[0].town') AS Town

FROM Person.Person

WHERE JSON_VALUE(jsonInfo, '$.info.address[0].state') like 'US%'

ORDER BY JSON_VALUE(jsonInfo, '$.info.address[0].town')

JSON_QUERY:

JSON_QUERY (expression [, path])

Example: The following example shows how to return a JSON fragment from CustomeFields column in query results.

SELECT PersonID, FullName,

JSON_QUERY(CustomFields, '$.OtherLanguages') AS Languages

FROM Application.People

JSON_MODIFY:

JSON_MODIFY (expression , path , newValue)

Example: The following example shows basic operations that can be done with JSON text.

DECLARE @info NVARCHAR(100) = '{"name":"John","skills":["C#","SQL"]}'

print @info

-- Update name

SET @info = JSON_MODIFY(@info, '$.name', 'Mike')

print @info

-- Insert surname

SET @info = JSON_MODIFY(@info, '$.surname', 'Smith')

print @info

-- Delete name

SET @info = JSON_MODIFY(@info, '$.name', NULL)

print @info

-- Add skill

SET @info = JSON_MODIFY(@info, 'append $.skills', 'Azure')

print @info

Resulting in:

{"name":"Nick","skills":["C#","SQL"]}

{"name":"John","skills":["C#","SQL"]}

{"name":"John","skills":["C#","SQL"],"surname":"Smith"}

{"skills":["C#","SQL"],"surname":"Smith"}

{"skills":["C#","SQL","Azure"],"surname":"Smith"}

CHOOSE:
CHOOSE (index, val_1, val_2 [, val_n])

Example: The following example returns the third item from the list of values that is provided.

SELECT CHOOSE (3, 'Manager', 'Director', 'Developer', 'Tester') AS Result;

Resulting in:

Result

Developer

(1 row(s) affected)

IIF:

IIF (boolean_expression, true_value, false_value)

Example: DECLARE @a int = 45, @b int = 40;

SELECT IIF (@a > @b, 'TRUE', 'FALSE') AS Result;

Resulting in:

Result

TRUE

(1 row(s) affected)

ABS:

-- Syntax for SQL Server, Azure SQL Database, Azure SQL Data Warehouse, Parallel Data Warehouse

ABS (numeric_expression)

Example: The following example shows the results of using the ABS function on three different numbers.

SELECT ABS(-1.0), ABS(0.0), ABS(1.0);

Resulting in:

---- ---- ----

1.0 .0 1.0

ACOS:

-- Syntax for SQL Server, Azure SQL Database, Azure SQL Data Warehouse, Parallel Data Warehouse

ACOS (float_expression)

Example:

The following example returns the ACOS of the specified number.

SET NOCOUNT OFF;

DECLARE @cos float;

SET @cos = -1.0;

SELECT 'The ACOS of the number is: ' + CONVERT(varchar, ACOS(@cos));

Resulting in:

The ACOS of the number is: 3.14159

(1 row(s) affected)

ASIN:

-- Syntax for SQL Server, Azure SQL Database, Azure SQL Data Warehouse, Parallel Data Warehouse

ASIN (float_expression)

Example: The following example takes a float expression and returns the ASIN of the specified angle.

/* The first value will be -1.01. This fails because the value is outside the range.*/

DECLARE @angle float

SET @angle = -1.01

SELECT 'The ASIN of the angle is: ' + CONVERT(varchar, ASIN(@angle))

GO

-- The next value is -1.00.

DECLARE @angle float

SET @angle = -1.00

SELECT 'The ASIN of the angle is: ' + CONVERT(varchar, ASIN(@angle))

GO

-- The next value is 0.1472738.

DECLARE @angle float

SET @angle = 0.1472738

SELECT 'The ASIN of the angle is: ' + CONVERT(varchar, ASIN(@angle))

GO

Resulting in:

.Net SqlClient Data Provider: Msg 3622, Level 16, State 1, Line 3

A domain error occurred.

The ASIN of the angle is: -1.5708

(1 row(s) affected)

The ASIN of the angle is: 0.147811

(1 row(s) affected)

ATAN:

-- Syntax for SQL Server, Azure SQL Database, Azure SQL Data Warehouse, Parallel Data Warehouse

ATAN (float_expression)

Example:

SELECT 'The ATAN of -45.01 is: ' + CONVERT(varchar, ATAN(-45.01))

SELECT 'The ATAN of -181.01 is: ' + CONVERT(varchar, ATAN(-181.01))

SELECT 'The ATAN of 0 is: ' + CONVERT(varchar, ATAN(0))

SELECT 'The ATAN of 0.1472738 is: ' + CONVERT(varchar, ATAN(0.1472738))

SELECT 'The ATAN of 197.1099392 is: ' + CONVERT(varchar, ATAN(197.1099392))

GO

Resulting in:

The ATAN of -45.01 is: -1.54858

(1 row(s) affected)

The ATAN of -181.01 is: -1.56527

(1 row(s) affected)

The ATAN of 0 is: 0

(1 row(s) affected)

The ATAN of 0.1472738 is: 0.146223

(1 row(s) affected)

The ATAN of 197.1099392 is: 1.56572

(1 row(s) affected)

ATN2:

-- Syntax for SQL Server, Azure SQL Database, Azure SQL Data Warehouse, Parallel Data Warehouse

ATN2 (float_expression , float_expression)

Example: DECLARE @x float = 35.175643, @y float = 129.44;

SELECT 'The ATN2 of the angle is: ' + CONVERT(varchar,ATN2(@x,@y));

GO

Resulting in:

The ATN2 of the angle is: 0.265345

(1 row(s) affected)

CEILING:

-- Syntax for SQL Server, Azure SQL Database, Azure SQL Data Warehouse, Parallel Data Warehouse

CEILING (numeric_expression)

Example: SELECT CEILING($123.45), CEILING($-123.45), CEILING($0.0);

GO

Resulting in:

--------- --------- ------------------------

124.00   -123.00   0.00

(1 row(s) affected)

COS:

-- Syntax for SQL Server, Azure SQL Database, Azure SQL Data Warehouse, Parallel Data Warehouse

COS (float_expression)

Example: DECLARE @angle float;

SET @angle = 14.78;

SELECT 'The COS of the angle is: ' + CONVERT(varchar,COS(@angle));

GO

Resulting in:

The COS of the angle is: -0.599465

(1 row(s) affected)

COT:

-- Syntax for SQL Server, Azure SQL Database, Azure SQL Data Warehouse, Parallel Data Warehouse

COT (float_expression)

Example:

DECLARE @angle float;

SET @angle = 124.1332;

SELECT 'The COT of the angle is: ' + CONVERT(varchar,COT(@angle));

GO

Resulting in:

The COT of the angle is: -0.040312

(1 row(s) affected)

DEGREES:

-- Syntax for SQL Server, Azure SQL Database, Azure SQL Data Warehouse, Parallel Data Warehouse

DEGREES (numeric_expression)

Example: SELECT 'The number of degrees in PI/2 radians is: '

+

CONVERT(varchar, DEGREES((PI()/2)));

GO

Resulting in:

The number of degrees in PI/2 radians is 90

(1 row(s) affected)

EXP:

-- Syntax for SQL Server, Azure SQL Database, Azure SQL Data Warehouse, Parallel Data Warehouse

EXP (float_expression)

Example: DECLARE @var float

SET @var = 10

```
SELECT  'The  EXP  of  the  variable  is:  '  +
CONVERT(varchar,EXP(@var))

GO
```

Resulting in:

```
-----------------------------------------------------------
```

The EXP of the variable is: 22026.5

(1 row(s) affected)

FLOOR:

-- Syntax for SQL Server, Azure SQL Data Warehouse, Parallel Data Warehouse

```
FLOOR ( numeric_expression )
```

Example: SELECT   FLOOR(123.45),   FLOOR(-123.45), FLOOR($123.45);

Resulting in:

```
---------    ---------    -----------
```

```
123        -124        123.0000
```

LOG:

-- Syntax for SQL Server

```
LOG ( float_expression [, base ] )
```

-- Syntax for Azure SQL Database, Azure SQL Data Warehouse, Parallel Data Warehouse

LOG (float_expression)

Example: The following example calculates the LOG for the specified float expression.

DECLARE @var float = 10;

SELECT 'The LOG of the variable is: ' + CONVERT(varchar, LOG(@var));

GO

Resulting in:

The LOG of the variable is: 2.30259

(1 row(s) affected)

LOG10:

-- Syntax for SQL Server, Azure SQL Database, Azure SQL Data Warehouse, Parallel Data Warehouse

LOG10 (float_expression)

Example: DECLARE @var float;

SET @var = 145.175643;

SELECT 'The LOG10 of the variable is: ' + CONVERT(varchar,LOG10(@var));

GO

Resulting in:

The LOG10 of the variable is: 2.16189

(1 row(s) affected)

PI:

-- Syntax for SQL Server, Azure SQL Database, Azure SQL Data Warehouse, Parallel Data Warehouse

PI ( )

Example: The following example returns the value of PI.

SELECT PI();

GO

Resulting in:

3.14159265358979

(1 row(s) affected)

POWER:

-- Syntax for SQL Server, Azure SQL Database, Azure SQL Data Warehouse, Parallel Data Warehouse

POWER (float_expression , y)

Example: The following example demonstrates raising a number to the power of 3 (the cube of the number).

DECLARE @input1 float;

DECLARE @input2 float;

SET @input1= 2;

SET @input2 = 2.5;

SELECT POWER(@input1, 3) AS Result1, POWER(@input2, 3) AS Result2;

Resulting in:

Result1   Result2

--------------------- ----------------------

8   15.625

(1 row(s) affected)

RADIANS:
-- Syntax for SQL Server, Azure SQL Database, Azure SQL Data Warehouse, Parallel Data Warehouse

RADIANS (numeric_expression)

Example: The following example takes a float expression and returns the RADIANS of the specified angle.

```
-- First value is -45.01.

DECLARE @angle float

SET @angle = -45.01

SELECT 'The RADIANS of the angle is: ' +

    CONVERT(varchar, RADIANS(@angle))

GO

-- Next value is -181.01.

DECLARE @angle float

SET @angle = -181.01

SELECT 'The RADIANS of the angle is: ' +

    CONVERT(varchar, RADIANS(@angle))

GO

-- Next value is 0.00.

DECLARE @angle float

SET @angle = 0.00

SELECT 'The RADIANS of the angle is: ' +

    CONVERT(varchar, RADIANS(@angle))

GO
```

-- Next value is 0.1472738.

DECLARE @angle float

SET @angle = 0.1472738

SELECT 'The RADIANS of the angle is: ' +

    CONVERT(varchar, RADIANS(@angle))

GO

-- Last value is 197.1099392.

DECLARE @angle float

SET @angle = 197.1099392

SELECT 'The RADIANS of the angle is: ' +

    CONVERT(varchar, RADIANS(@angle))

GO

Resulting in:

The RADIANS of the angle is: -0.785573

(1 row(s) affected)

The RADIANS of the angle is: -3.15922

(1 row(s) affected)

The RADIANS of the angle is: 0

(1 row(s) affected)

The RADIANS of the angle is: 0.00257041

 (1 row(s) affected)

The RADIANS of the angle is: 3.44022

(1 row(s) affected)

RAND:

RAND ([seed])

Example: The following example produces four different random numbers that are generated by the RAND function.

DECLARE @counter smallint;

SET @counter = 1;

WHILE @counter < 5

  BEGIN

    SELECT RAND() Random_Number

SET @counter = @counter + 1

END;

GO

ROUND:

-- Syntax for SQL Server and Azure SQL Database

ROUND (numeric_expression , length [,function])

-- Syntax for Azure SQL Data Warehouse and Parallel Data Warehouse

ROUND (numeric_expression , length)

Example: The following example shows two expressions that demonstrate by using ROUND the last digit is always an estimate.

SELECT ROUND(123.9994, 3), ROUND(123.9995, 3);

GO

Resulting in:

----------- -----------

123.9990   124.0000

SIGN:

-- Syntax for SQL Server, Azure SQL Database, Azure SQL Data Warehouse, Parallel Data Warehouse

SIGN (numeric_expression)

Example: The following example returns the SIGN values of numbers from -1 to 1.

```
DECLARE @value real

SET @value = -1

WHILE @value < 2

  BEGIN

    SELECT SIGN(@value)

    SET NOCOUNT ON

    SELECT @value = @value + 1

    SET NOCOUNT OFF

  END

SET NOCOUNT OFF

GO
```

Resulting in:

(1 row(s) affected)

-1.0

(1 row(s) affected)

0.0

(1 row(s) affected)

1.0

(1 row(s) affected)

SIN:

-- Syntax for SQL Server, Azure SQL Database, Azure SQL Data Warehouse, Parallel Data Warehouse

SIN (float_expression)

Example: The following example calculates the SIN for a specified angle.

DECLARE @angle float;

SET @angle = 45.175643;

SELECT 'The SIN of the angle is: ' + CONVERT(varchar,SIN(@angle));

GO

Resulting in:

The SIN of the angle is: 0.929607

(1 row(s) affected)

SORT:

-- Syntax for SQL Server, Azure SQL Database, Azure SQL Data Warehouse, Parallel Data Warehouse

SQRT (float_expression)

Example: The following example returns the square root of numbers between 1.00 and 10.00.

DECLARE @myvalue float;

SET @myvalue = 1.00;

WHILE @myvalue < 10.00

  BEGIN

    SELECT SQRT(@myvalue);

    SET @myvalue = @myvalue + 1

  END;

GO

Resulting in:

1.0

1.4142135623731

1.73205080756888

2.0

2.23606797749979

2.44948974278318

2.64575131106459

2.82842712474619

3.0

SQUARE:

-- Syntax for SQL Server, Azure SQL Data Warehouse, Parallel Data Warehouse

SQUARE (float_expression)

Example: The following example returns the volume of a cylinder having a radius of 1 inch and a height of 5 inches.

DECLARE @h float, @r float;

SET @h = 5;

SET @r = 1;

SELECT PI()* SQUARE(@r)* @h AS 'Cyl Vol';

Resulting in:

Cyl Vol

15.707963267948966

TAN:

-- Syntax for SQL Server, Azure SQL Database, Azure SQL Data Warehouse, Parallel Data Warehouse

TAN (float_expression)

Example: The following example returns the tangent of PI()/2

SELECT TAN(PI()/2);

Results in:

1.6331778728383844E+16

@@PROCID:

Example: The following example uses @@PROCID as the input parameter in the OBJECT_NAME function to return the name of the stored procedure in the RAISERROR message.

```
USE AdventureWorks2012;

GO

IF OBJECT_ID ( 'usp_FindName', 'P' ) IS NOT NULL

DROP PROCEDURE usp_FindName;

GO

CREATE PROCEDURE usp_FindName

    @lastname varchar(40) = '%',

    @firstname varchar(20) = '%'

AS

DECLARE @Count int;

DECLARE @ProcName nvarchar(128);

SELECT LastName, FirstName

FROM Person.Person

WHERE FirstName LIKE @firstname AND LastName LIKE @lastname;
```

```
SET @Count = @@ROWCOUNT;

SET @ProcName = OBJECT_NAME(@@PROCID);

RAISERROR ('Stored procedure %s returned %d rows.', 16,10,
@ProcName, @Count);

GO

EXECUTE dbo.usp_FindName 'P%', 'A%';
```

APP_NAME:

```
APP_NAME ( )
```

Example: The following example checks whether the client application that initiated this process is a SQL Server Management Studio session and provides a date in either US or ANSI format.

```
USE AdventureWorks2012;

GO

IF APP_NAME() = 'Microsoft SQL Server Management
Studio - Query'

PRINT 'This process was started by ' + APP_NAME() + '. The
date is ' + CONVERT ( varchar(100) , GETDATE(), 101) + '.';

ELSE

PRINT 'This process was started by ' + APP_NAME() + '. The
date is ' + CONVERT ( varchar(100) , GETDATE(), 102) + '.';
```

APPLOCK_MODE:

APPLOCK_MODE('database_principal' , 'resource_name' , 'lock_owner')

Example: Two users (User A and User B) with separate sessions run the following sequence of Transact-SQL statements.

User A Runs:

```
USE AdventureWorks2012;

GO

BEGIN TRAN;

DECLARE @result int;

EXEC @result=sp_getapplock

    @DbPrincipal='public',

    @Resource='Form1',

    @LockMode='Shared',

    @LockOwner='Transaction';

SELECT APPLOCK_MODE('public', 'Form1', 'Transaction');

GO
```

User B then runs:

```
Use AdventureWorks2012;
```

```
GO

BEGIN TRAN;

SELECT APPLOCK_MODE('public', 'Form1', 'Transaction');

--Result set: NoLock

SELECT   APPLOCK_TEST('public',   'Form1',   'Shared',
'Transaction');

--Result set: 1 (Lock is grantable.)

SELECT   APPLOCK_TEST('public',   'Form1',   'Exclusive',
'Transaction');

--Result set: 0 (Lock is not grantable.)

GO
```

User A then runs:

```
EXEC           sp_releaseapplock           @Resource='Form1',
@DbPrincipal='public';

GO
```

User B then runs:

```
SELECT   APPLOCK_TEST('public',   'Form1',   'Exclusive',
'Transaction');

--Result set: '1' (The lock is grantable.)
```

GO

User A and B then run:

COMMIT TRAN;

GO

APPLOCK_TEST:
APPLOCK_TEST ('database_principal' , 'resource_name' , 'lock_mode' , 'lock_owner')

Example: In the following example, two users (User A and User B) with separate sessions run the following sequence of Transact-SQL statements.

User A runs:

USE AdventureWorks2012;

GO

BEGIN TRAN;

DECLARE @result int;

EXEC @result=sp_getapplock

    @DbPrincipal='public',

    @Resource='Form1',

    @LockMode='Shared',

```
                    @LockOwner='Transaction';

         SELECT APPLOCK_MODE('public', 'Form1', 'Transaction');

         GO

         User B runs:

         Use AdventureWorks2012;

         GO

         BEGIN TRAN;

         SELECT APPLOCK_MODE('public', 'Form1', 'Transaction');

         --Result set: NoLock

         SELECT      APPLOCK_TEST('public',   'Form1',   'Shared',
         'Transaction');

         --Result set: 1 (Lock is grantable.)

         SELECT      APPLOCK_TEST('public',   'Form1',   'Exclusive',
         'Transaction');

         --Result set: 0 (Lock is not grantable.)

         GO

         User A then runs:

         EXEC          sp_releaseapplock          @Resource='Form1',
         @DbPrincipal='public';
```

GO

User B then runs:

SELECT   APPLOCK_TEST('public',   'Form1',   'Exclusive',
'Transaction');

--Result set: '1' (The lock is grantable.)

GO

User A and B then run:

COMMIT TRAN;

GO

ASSEMBLYPROPERTY:
ASSEMBLYPROPERTY('assembly_name', 'property_name')

Example: The following example assumes a HelloWorld assembly is registered in the AdventureWorks2012 database.

USE AdventureWorks2012;

GO

SELECT   ASSEMBLYPROPERTY   ('HelloWorld'   ,
'PublicKey');

COL_LENGTH:
COL_LENGTH ('table' , 'column')

Example: The following example shows the return values for a column of type varchar(40) and a column of type nvarchar(40)

USE AdventureWorks2012;

GO

CREATE TABLE t1(c1 varchar(40), c2 nvarchar(40));

GO

SELECT COL_LENGTH('t1','c1')AS 'VarChar',

  COL_LENGTH('t1','c2')AS 'NVarChar';

GO

DROP TABLE t1;

Results in:

VarChar   NVarChar

40   80

COL_NAME:

-- Syntax for SQL Server, Azure SQL Database, Azure SQL Data Warehouse, Parallel Data Warehouse

COL_NAME (table_id , column_id)

Example: The following example returns the name of the first column in the Employee table of the AdventureWorks2012 database.

```sql
USE AdventureWorks2012;

GO

SET NOCOUNT OFF;

GO

SELECT
COL_NAME(OBJECT_ID('HumanResources.Employee'),    1)    AS
'Column Name';

GO
```

Results in:

Column Name

BusinessEntityID

COLUMNPROPERTY:

COLUMNPROPERTY (id , column , property)

Example: The following example returns the length of the LastName column.

```sql
USE AdventureWorks2012;

GO
```

SELECT COLUMNPROPERTY(

OBJECT_ID('Person.Person'),'LastName','PRECISION')AS 'Column Length';

GO

Results in:

Column Length

50

DATABASE_PRINCIPAL_ID:
DATABASE_PRINCIPAL_ID ('principal_name')

Example: The following example returns the database principal ID of the current user.

SELECT DATABASE_PRINCIPAL_ID();

GO

DATABASEPROPERTYVEX:
-- Syntax for SQL Server, Azure SQL Database, Azure SQL Data Warehouse, Parallel Data Warehouse

DATABASEPROPERTYEX (database , property)

Example: The following example returns several attributes of the AdventureWorks database.

SELECT

DATABASEPROPERTYEX('AdventureWorks2014', 'Collation') AS Collation,

DATABASEPROPERTYEX('AdventureWorks2014', 'Edition') AS Edition,

DATABASEPROPERTYEX('AdventureWorks2014', 'ServiceObjective') AS ServiceObjective,

DATABASEPROPERTYEX('AdventureWorks2014', 'MaxSizeInBytes') AS MaxSizeInBytes

Resulting in:

Collation   Edition   ServiceObjective
MaxSizeInBytes

---------------------------- ------------- ---------------- --------------

SQL_Latin1_General_CP1_CI_AS DataWarehouse DW1000
5368709120

DB_ID:
-- Syntax for SQL Server, Azure SQL Database, Azure SQL Data Warehouse, Parallel Data Warehouse

DB_ID (['database_name'])

Example: The following example returns the database ID of the current database.

SELECT DB_ID() AS [Database ID];

GO

DB_NAME:

-- Syntax for SQL Server, Azure SQL Database, Azure SQL Data Warehouse, Parallel Data Warehouse

DB_NAME ([database_id]

Example: The following example returns the name of the current database

SELECT DB_NAME() AS [Current Database];

GO

FILE_ID:

FILE_ID (file_name)

Example: The following example returns the file ID for the AdventureWorks_Data file.

USE AdventureWorks2012;

GO

SELECT FILE_ID('AdventureWorks2012_Data')AS 'File ID';

GO

Resulting in:

File ID

1

(1 row(s) affected)

FILE_IDEX:

FILE_IDEX (file_name)

Example: The following example returns the file ID for the AdventureWorks_Data file.

USE AdventureWorks2012;

GO

SELECT FILE_IDEX('AdventurcWorks2012_Data')AS 'File ID';

GO

Resulting in:

File ID

1

(1 row(s) affected)

FILE_NAME:

FILE_NAME (file_name)

Example: The following example returns the file names for file_ID 1 and file_ID in the AdventureWorks2012 database.

SELECT FILE_NAME(1) AS 'File Name 1', FILE_NAME(2) AS 'File Name 2';

GO

Resulting in:

File Name 1 File Name 2

---------------- ------------------------

AdventureWorks2012_Data AdventureWorks2012_Log

(1 row(s) affected)

FILEGROUP_ID:
FILEGROUP_ID ('filegroup_name')

Example: The following example returns the filegroup ID for the filegroup named PRIMARY in the AdventureWorks2012 database

SELECT FILEGROUP_ID('PRIMARY') AS [Filegroup ID];

GO

Resulting in:

Filegroup ID

1

(1 row(s) affected)

FILEGROUP_NAME:

FILEGROUP_NAME (filegroup_id)

Example: The following example returns the filegroup name for the filegroup ID 1 in the AdventureWorks2012 database.

SELECT FILEGROUP_NAME(1) AS [Filegroup Name];

GO

Resulting in:

Filegroup Name

PRIMARY

(1 row(s) affected)

FILEGROUPPROPERTY:

FILEGROUPPROPERTY (filegroup_name , property)

Example: This example returns the setting for the IsDefault property for the primary filegroup in the AdventureWorks2012 database.

SELECT FILEGROUPPROPERTY('PRIMARY', 'IsDefault') AS 'Default Filegroup';

GO

Resulting in:

Default Filegroup

1

(1 row(s) affected)

FILEPROPERTY:

FILEPROPERTY (file_name , property)

Example: The following example returns the setting for the IsPrimaryFile property for the AdventureWorks_Data file name in AdventureWorks2012 the database.

SELECT   FILEPROPERTY('AdventureWorks2012_Data', 'IsPrimaryFile')AS [Primary File];

GO

Resulting in:

Primary File

1

(1 row(s) affected)

FULLTEXTCATALOGPROPERTY:

FULLTEXTCATALOGPROPERTY ('catalog_name' ,'property')

Something to keep in mind with this function per Microsoft, "FULLTEXTCATALOGPROPERTY ('catalog_name','IndexSize') looks at only fragments with status 4 or 6 as shown in sys.fulltext_index_fragments. These fragments are part of the logical index. Therefore, the IndexSize property returns only the logical index size. During an index merge, however, the actual index size might be double its logical size. To find the actual size that is being consumed by a full-text index during a merge, use the sp_spaceused system stored procedure. That procedure looks at all fragments associated with a full-text index. If you restrict the growth of the full-text catalog file and do not allow enough space for the merge process, the full-text population may fail. In this case, FULLTEXTCATALOGPROPERTY ('catalog_name' ,'IndexSize') returns 0 and the following error is written to the full-text log:

Error: 30059, Severity: 16, State: 1. A fatal error occurred during a full-text population and caused the population to be cancelled. Population type is: FULL; database name is FTS_Test (id: 13); catalog name is t1_cat (id: 5); table name t1 (id: 2105058535). Fix the errors that are logged in the full-text crawl log. Then, resume the population. The basic Transact-SQL syntax for this is: ALTER FULLTEXT INDEX ON table_name RESUME POPULATION.

It is important that applications do not wait in a tight loop, checking for the PopulateStatus property to become idle (indicating that population has completed) because this takes CPU cycles away from the database and full-text search processes, and causes timeouts. In addition, it is usually a better option to check the corresponding PopulateStatus property at the table level, TableFullTextPopulateStatus in the OBJECTPROPERTYEX system function. This and other new full-text properties in OBJECTPROPERTYEX provide more granular information about full-text indexing tables. For more information, see OBJECTPROPERTYEX (Transact-SQL)."

Example: The following example returns the number of full-text indexed items in a full-text catalog named Cat_Desc.

USE AdventureWorks2012;

GO

SELECT fulltextcatalogproperty('Cat_Desc', 'ItemCount');

GO

FULLTEXTSERVICEPROPERTY:
FULLTEXTSERVICEPROPERTY ('property')

Example: The following example checks whether only signed binaries are loaded, and the return value indicates that this verification is not occurring.

SELECT fulltextserviceproperty('VerifySignature');

Resulting in:

```
-----------

       0
```

INDEX_COL: (Microsoft, 2014)

INDEX_COL ('[database_name . [schema_name] .| schema_name]

  table_or_view_name', index_id , key_id)

Example: The following example returns the column names of the two key columns in the index PK_SalesOrderDetail_SalesOrderID_LineNumber.

USE AdventureWorks2012;

GO

SELECT

  INDEX_COL (N'AdventureWorks2012.Sales.SalesOrderDetail', 1,1) AS

    [Index Column 1],

  INDEX_COL (N'AdventureWorks2012.Sales.SalesOrderDetail', 1,2) AS

    [Index Column 2]

  ;

GO

Resulting in:

```
Index Column 1     Index Column 2

-------------------------------------------------

SalesOrderID       SalesOrderDetailID
```

INDEXKEY_PROPERTY:

INDEXKEY_PROPERTY (object_ID ,index_ID ,key_ID ,property)

Example: In the following example, both properties are returned for index ID 1, key column 1 in the Production.Location table.

USE AdventureWorks2012;

GO

SELECT

INDEXKEY_PROPERTY(OBJECT_ID('Production.Location', 'U'),

1,1,'ColumnId') AS [Column ID],

INDEXKEY_PROPERTY(OBJECT_ID('Production.Location', 'U'),

1,1,'IsDescending') AS [Asc or Desc order];

Resulting in:

```
Column ID   Asc or Desc order

----------- -----------------
```

```
1        0
```

(1 row(s) affected)

INDEXPROPERTY:

-- Syntax for SQL Server, Azure SQL Database, Azure SQL Data Warehouse, Parallel Data Warehouse

INDEXPROPERTY (object_ID , index_or_statistics_name , property)

Example: The following example returns the values for the IsClustered, IndexDepth, and IndexFillFactor properties for the PK_Employee_BusinessEntityID index of the Employee table in the AdventureWorks2012 database.

SELECT

INDEXPROPERTY(OBJECT_ID('HumanResources.Employee'),

'PK_Employee_BusinessEntityID','IsClustered')AS [Is Clustered],

INDEXPROPERTY(OBJECT_ID('HumanResources.Employee'),

'PK_Employee_BusinessEntityID','IndexDepth') AS [Index Depth],

INDEXPROPERTY(OBJECT_ID('HumanResources.Employee'),

'PK_Employee_BusinessEntityID','IndexFillFactor')   AS [Fill Factor];

Resulting in:

Is Clustered Index Depth Fill Factor

------------ ----------- -----------

1   2   0

(1 row(s) affected)

NEXT VALUE FOR:

NEXT VALUE FOR [database_name .] [schema_name .] sequence_name

[OVER (<over_order_by_clause>)]

- Things to keep in mind are some restrictions for this function.

- The NEXT VALUE FOR function cannot be used in the following situations:

- When a database is in read-only mode.

- As an argument to a table-valued function.

- As an argument to an aggregate function.

- In subqueries including common table expressions and derived tables.

- In views, in user-defined functions, or in computed columns.

- In a statement using the DISTINCT, UNION, UNION ALL, EXCEPT or INTERSECT operator.

- In a statement using the ORDER BY clause unless NEXT VALUE FOR … OVER (ORDER BY …) is used.

- In the following clauses: FETCH, OVER, OUTPUT, ON, PIVOT, UNPIVOT, GROUP BY, HAVING, COMPUTE, COMPUTE BY, or FOR XML.

- In conditional expressions using CASE, CHOOSE, COALESCE, IIF, ISNULL, or NULLIF.

- In a VALUES clause that is not part of an INSERT statement.

- In the definition of a check constraint.

- In the definition of a rule or default object. (It can be used in a default constraint.)

- As a default in a user-defined table type.

- In a statement using TOP, OFFSET, or when the ROWCOUNT option is set.

- In the WHERE clause of a statement.

- In a MERGE statement. (Except when the NEXT VALUE FOR function is used in a default constraint in the target table and default is used in the CREATE statement of the MERGE statement.)

Example: The following examples use a sequence named CountBy1 in a schema named Test. Execute the following statement to create the Test.CountBy1 sequence. Examples C and E use the AdventureWorks2012 database, so the CountBy1 sequence is created in that database.

USE AdventureWorks2012 ;

GO

CREATE SCHEMA Test;

GO

CREATE SEQUENCE Test.CountBy1

START WITH 1

INCREMENT BY 1 ;

GO

OBJECT_DEFINITION:
OBJECT_DEFINITION (object_id)

Example: The following example returns the definition of a user-defined trigger, uAddress, in the Person schema. The built-in function OBJECT_ID is used to return the object ID of the trigger to the OBJECT_DEFINITION statement.

USE AdventureWorks2012;

GO

SELECT OBJECT_DEFINITION (OBJECT_ID(N'Person.uAddress')) AS [Trigger Definition];

GO

OBJECT_ID:
-- Syntax for SQL Server, Azure SQL Database, Azure SQL Data Warehouse, Parallel Data Warehouse

OBJECT_ID ('[database_name . [schema_name] . | schema_name .]

object_name' [,'object_type'])

Example: The following example returns the object ID for the Production.WorkOrder table in the AdventureWorks2012 database.

USE master;

GO

SELECT OBJECT_ID(N'AdventureWorks2012.Production.WorkOrder') AS 'Object ID';

GO

OBJECT_NAME:

-- Syntax for SQL Server, Azure SQL Database, Azure SQL Data Warehouse, Parallel Data Warehouse

OBJECT_NAME (object_id [, database_id])

Example: The following example returns columns from the sys.objects catalog view for the object specified by OBJECT_NAME in the WHERE clause of the SELECT statement.

USE AdventureWorks2012;

GO

DECLARE @MyID int;

SET @MyID = (SELECT OBJECT_ID('AdventureWorks2012.Production.Product',

'U'));

SELECT name, object_id, type_desc

FROM sys.objects

WHERE name = OBJECT_NAME(@MyID);

GO

OBJECT_SCHEMA_NAME:

OBJECT_SCHEMA_NAME (object_id [, database_id])

Example: The following example returns the object schema name, object name, and SQL text for all cached query plans that are not ad hoc or prepared statements.

```
SELECT DB_NAME(st.dbid) AS database_name,

    OBJECT_SCHEMA_NAME(st.objectid,    st.dbid)    AS
schema_name,

    OBJECT_NAME(st.objectid, st.dbid) AS object_name,

    st.text AS query_statement

FROM sys.dm_exec_query_stats AS qs

CROSS APPLY sys.dm_exec_sql_text(qs.sql_handle) AS st

WHERE st.objectid IS NOT NULL;

GO
```

OBJECTPROPERTY:

```
-- Syntax for SQL Server, Azure SQL Database, Azure SQL Data
Warehouse, Parallel Data Warehouse

OBJECTPROPERTY ( id , property )
```

Example: The following example tests whether UnitMeasure is a table in the AdventureWorks2012 database.

```
USE AdventureWorks2012;

GO
```

```
IF OBJECTPROPERTY
(OBJECT_ID(N'Production.UnitMeasure'),'ISTABLE') = 1

    PRINT 'UnitMeasure is a table.'

ELSE IF OBJECTPROPERTY
(OBJECT_ID(N'Production.UnitMeasure'),'ISTABLE') = 0

    PRINT 'UnitMeasure is not a table.'

ELSE IF OBJECTPROPERTY
(OBJECT_ID(N'Production.UnitMeasure'),'ISTABLE') IS NULL

    PRINT 'ERROR: UnitMeasure is not a valid object.';

GO
```

OBJECTPROPERTYEX:

-- Syntax for SQL Server, Azure SQL Database, Azure SQL Data Warehouse, Parallel Data Warehouse

```
OBJECTPROPERTYEX ( id , property )
```

Example: The following example creates a SYNONYM MyEmployeeTable for the Employee table in the AdventureWorks2012 database and then returns the base type of the SYNONYM.

```
USE AdventureWorks2012;

GO
```

CREATE SYNONYM MyEmployeeTable FOR HumanResources.Employee;

GO

SELECT OBJECTPROPERTYEX (
object_id(N'MyEmployeeTable'), N'BaseType')AS [Base Type];

GO

Results in:

Base Type

U

ORIGINAL_DB_NAME:
ORIGINAL_DB_NAME ()

PARSENAME:
-- Syntax for SQL Server, Azure SQL Database, Azure SQL Data Warehouse, Parallel Data Warehouse

PARSENAME ('object_name' , object_piece)

Example: The following example uses PARSENAME to return information about the Person table in the AdventureWorks2012 database.

USE AdventureWorks2012;

```
        SELECT   PARSENAME('AdventureWorks2012..Person',  1)
AS 'Object Name';

        SELECT   PARSENAME('AdventureWorks2012..Person',  2)
AS 'Schema Name';

        SELECT   PARSENAME('AdventureWorks2012..Person',  3)
AS 'Database Name';

        SELECT   PARSENAME('AdventureWorks2012..Person',  4)
AS 'Server Name';

    GO

    Resulting in:

    Object Name

    ----------------------------

    Person

    (1 row(s) affected)

    Schema Name

    ----------------------------

    (null)

    (1 row(s) affected)

    Database Name
```

AdventureWorks2012

(1 row(s) affected)

Server Name

(null)

(1 row(s) affected)

SCHEMA_ID:

-- Syntax for SQL Server, Azure SQL Database, Azure SQL Data Warehouse, Parallel Data Warehouse

SCHEMA_ID ([schema_name])

Example:

SELECT SCHEMA_ID();

GO

SCHEMA_NAME:

-- Syntax for SQL Server, Azure SQL Database, Azure SQL Data Warehouse, Parallel Data Warehouse

SCHEMA_NAME ([schema_id])

SCOPE_IDENTITY: (Microsoft, 2012)

SCOPE_IDENTITY()

Example:

The following example creates two tables, TZ and TY, and an INSERT trigger on TZ. When a row is inserted to table TZ, the trigger (Ztrig) fires and inserts a row in TY.

```
USE tempdb;

GO

CREATE TABLE TZ (

    Z_id  int IDENTITY(1,1)PRIMARY KEY,

    Z_name varchar(20) NOT NULL);

INSERT TZ

    VALUES ('Lisa'),('Mike'),('Carla');

SELECT * FROM TZ;

--Result set: This is how table TZ looks.

Z_id Z_name

-------------

1 Lisa

2 Mike

3 Carla

CREATE TABLE TY (
```

```sql
Y_id  int IDENTITY(100,5)PRIMARY KEY,

Y_name varchar(20) NULL);

INSERT TY (Y_name)

VALUES ('boathouse'), ('rocks'), ('elevator');

SELECT * FROM TY;

--Result set: This is how TY looks:

Y_id Y_name

---------------

100 boathouse

105 rocks

110 elevator

/*Create the trigger that inserts a row in table TY

when a row is inserted in table TZ.*/

CREATE TRIGGER Ztrig

ON TZ

FOR INSERT AS

  BEGIN

  INSERT TY VALUES ('')
```

END;

/*FIRE the trigger and determine what identity values you obtain

with the @@IDENTITY and SCOPE_IDENTITY functions.*/

INSERT TZ VALUES ('Rosalie');

SELECT SCOPE_IDENTITY() AS [SCOPE_IDENTITY];

GO

SELECT @@IDENTITY AS [@@IDENTITY];

GO

Resulting in:

SCOPE_IDENTITY

4

/*SCOPE_IDENTITY returned the last identity value in the same scope. This was the insert on table TZ.*/

@@IDENTITY

115

/*@@IDENTITY returned the last identity value inserted to TY by the trigger. This fired because of an earlier insert on TZ.*/

SERVERPROPERTY:

-- Syntax for SQL Server, Azure SQL Database, Azure SQL Data Warehouse, Parallel Data Warehouse

SERVERPROPERTY (propertyname)

Example: The following example uses the SERVERPROPERTY function in a SELECT statement to return information about the current server. This scenario is useful when there are multiple instances of SQL Server installed on a Windows server, and the client must open another connection to the same instance used by the current connection.

SELECT   CONVERT(sysname, SERVERPROPERTY('servername'));

GO

The following example uses the SERVERPROPERTY function in a SELECT statement to return version information about the product.

SELECT

SERVERPROPERTY('ProductVersion') AS ProductVersion,

SERVERPROPERTY('ProductLevel') AS ProductLevel,

SERVERPROPERTY('Edition') AS Edition,

SERVERPROPERTY('EngineEdition') AS EngineEdition;

GO

STATS_DATE:

-- Syntax for SQL Server, Azure SQL Database, Azure SQL Data Warehouse, Parallel Data Warehouse

STATS_DATE (object_id , stats_id)

Example: The following example returns the date of the most recent update for each statistics object on the Person.Address table.

USE AdventureWorks2012;

GO

SELECT name AS stats_name,

STATS_DATE(object_id,   stats_id)   AS statistics_update_date

FROM sys.stats

WHERE object_id = OBJECT_ID('Person.Address');

GO

If statistics correspond to an index, the stats_id value in the sys.stats catalog view is the same as the index_id value in the sys.indexes catalog view, and the following query returns the same results as the preceding query. If statistics do not correspond to an index, they are in the sys.stats results but not in the sys.indexes results.

USE AdventureWorks2012;

GO

SELECT name AS index_name,

STATS_DATE(object_id,   index_id)   AS
statistics_update_date

FROM sys.indexes

WHERE object_id = OBJECT_ID('Person.Address');

GO

TYPE_ID:

-- Syntax for SQL Server, Azure SQL Database, Azure SQL Data
Warehouse, Parallel Data Warehouse

TYPE_ID ([schema_name] type_name)

Example: The following example returns type ID for single-
and two-part type names.

USE tempdb;

GO

CREATE TYPE NewType FROM int;

GO

CREATE SCHEMA NewSchema;

GO

```sql
CREATE TYPE NewSchema.NewType FROM int;

GO

SELECT TYPE_ID('NewType') AS [1 Part Data Type ID],

    TYPE_ID('NewSchema.NewType') AS [2 Part Data Type ID];

GO
```

TYPE_NAME:

-- Syntax for SQL Server, Azure SQL Database, Azure SQL Data Warehouse, Parallel Data Warehouse

```sql
TYPE_NAME ( type_id )
```

Example: The following example returns the object name, column name, and type name for each column in the Vendor table of the AdventureWorks2012 database.

```sql
SELECT o.name AS obj_name, c.name AS col_name,

    TYPE_NAME(c.user_type_id) AS type_name

FROM sys.objects AS o

JOIN sys.columns AS c  ON o.object_id = c.object_id

WHERE o.name = 'Vendor'

ORDER BY col_name;

GO
```

Resulting in:

obj_name col_name type_name

--------------- ------------------------ --------------

Vendor AccountNumber AccountNumber

Vendor ActiveFlag Flag

Vendor BusinessEntityID int

Vendor CreditRating tinyint

Vendor ModifiedDate datetime

Vendor Name Name

Vendor PreferredVendorStatus Flag

Vendor PurchasingWebServiceURL nvarchar

(8 row(s) affected)

TYPEPROPERTY:
-- Syntax for SQL Server, Azure SQL Database, Azure SQL Data Warehouse, Parallel Data Warehouse

TYPEPROPERTY (type , property)

Example: The following example returns the owner of a data type.

```sql
SELECT TYPEPROPERTY(SCHEMA_NAME(schema_id) +
'.' + name, 'OwnerId') AS owner_id, name, system_type_id,
user_type_id, schema_id

FROM sys.types;
```

VERSION:

```sql
-- Azure SQL Data Warehouse and Parallel Data Warehouse

VERSION ( )
```

Example: The following example returns the version number.

```sql
SELECT VERSION();
```

CERTENCODED:

```sql
CERTENCODED ( cert_id )
```

Example: The following example creates a certificate named Shipping04 and then uses the CERTENCODED function to return the binary encoding of the certificate.

```sql
CREATE DATABASE TEST1;

GO

USE TEST1

CREATE CERTIFICATE Shipping04

ENCRYPTION BY PASSWORD =
'pGFD4bb925DGvbd2439587y'
```

```
WITH SUBJECT = 'Sammamish Shipping Records',

EXPIRY_DATE = '20161031';

GO

SELECT CERTENCODED(CERT_ID('Shipping04'));
```

CERTPRIVATEKEY:
```
CERTPRIVATEKEY

    (

        cert_ID

        , ' encryption_password '

        [ , ' decryption_password ' ]

    )
```

Example:

```
CREATE DATABASE TEST1;

GO

USE TEST1

CREATE MASTER KEY ENCRYPTION BY PASSWORD =
'Use 5tr0ng P^55Words'

GO

CREATE CERTIFICATE Shipping04
```

WITH SUBJECT = 'Sammamish Shipping Records',

EXPIRY_DATE = '20141031';

GO

SELECT   CERTPRIVATEKEY(CERT_ID('Shipping04'),
'jklalkaa/; uia3dd');

CURRENT_USER:
-- Syntax for SQL Server, Azure SQL Database, Azure SQL Data
Warehouse, Parallel Data Warehouse

CURRENT_USER

Example: The following example returns the name of the
current user.

SELECT CURRENT_USER;

GO

Second Example: The following example creates a table that
uses CURRENT_USER as a DEFAULT constraint for the order
person column on a sales row.

USE AdventureWorks2012;

GO

IF   EXISTS   (SELECT   TABLE_NAME   FROM
INFORMATION_SCHEMA.TABLES

```
        WHERE TABLE_NAME = 'orders22')

    DROP TABLE orders22;

GO

SET NOCOUNT ON;

CREATE TABLE orders22

(

    order_id int IDENTITY(1000, 1) NOT NULL,

    cust_id  int NOT NULL,

    order_date    smalldatetime    NOT    NULL    DEFAULT
GETDATE(),

    order_amt money NOT NULL,

    order_person    char(30)    NOT    NULL    DEFAULT
CURRENT_USER

    );

    GO
```

The following code inserts a record in the table. The user that is executing these statements is named

Wanida.

```
INSERT orders22 (cust_id, order_amt)
```

VALUES (5105, 577.95);

GO

SET NOCOUNT OFF;

GO

The following query selects all information from the orders22 table.

SELECT * FROM orders22;

GO

Resulting in:

order_id cust_id order_date order_amt order_person

----------- ----------- -------------------- ----------- -----------

1000 5105 2005-04-03 23:34:00 577.95 Wanida

(1 row(s) affected)

HAS_DBACCESS:

-- Syntax for SQL Server, Azure SQL Data Warehouse, Parallel Data Warehouse

HAS_DBACCESS ('database_name')

Example: The following example tests whether current user has access to the AdventureWorks2012 database.

SELECT HAS_DBACCESS('AdventureWorks2012');

GO

HAS_PERMS_BY_NAME:
HAS_PERMS_BY_NAME (securable , securable_class , permission

[, sub-securable] [, sub-securable_class])

Some important remarks on this built in function per Microsoft, "This built-in function tests whether the current principal has a particular effective permission on a specified securable. HAS_PERMS_BY_NAME returns 1 when the user has effective permission on the securable, 0 when the user has no effective permission on the securable, and NULL when the securable class or permission is not valid. An effective permission is any of the following:

- A permission granted directly to the principal, and not denied.

- A permission implied by a higher-level permission held by the principal and not denied.

- A permission granted to a role or group of which the principal is a member, and not denied.

- A permission held by a role or group of which the principal is a member, and not denied.

The permission evaluation is always performed in the security context of the caller. To determine whether some other user has an effective permission, the caller must have IMPERSONATE permission on that user.

For schema-level entities, one-, two-, or three-part nonnull names are accepted. For database-level entities a one-part name is accepted, with a null value meaning "current database". For the server itself, a null value (meaning "current server") is required. This function cannot check permissions on a linked server or on a Windows user for which no server-level principal has been created."

IS_MEMBER:
IS_MEMBER ({ 'group' | 'role' })

Example: The following example checks whether the current user is a member of a database role or a Windows domain group.

```
-- Test membership in db_owner and print appropriate
message.

IF IS_MEMBER ('db_owner') = 1

  PRINT 'Current user is a member of the db_owner role'

ELSE IF IS_MEMBER ('db_owner') = 0

  PRINT 'Current user is NOT a member of the db_owner role'

ELSE IF IS_MEMBER ('db_owner') IS NULL

  PRINT 'ERROR: Invalid group / role specified';

GO
```

-- Execute SELECT if user is a member of ADVWORKS\Shipping.

IF IS_MEMBER ('ADVWORKS\Shipping') = 1

SELECT 'User ' + USER + ' is a member of ADVWORKS\Shipping.';

GO

IS_ROLEMASTER:
IS_ROLEMEMBER ('role' [, 'database_principal'])

Example: The following example indicates whether the current user is a member of the db_datareader fixed database role.

IF IS_ROLEMEMBER ('db_datareader') = 1

print 'Current user is a member of the db_datareader role'

ELSE IF IS_ROLEMEMBER ('db_datareader') = 0

print 'Current user is NOT a member of the db_datareader role'

ELSE IF IS_ROLEMEMBER ('db_datareader') IS NULL

print 'ERROR: The database role specified is not valid.';

IS_SRVROLEMEMBER:
IS_SRVROLEMEMBER ('role' [, 'login'])

Example: The following example indicates whether the SQL Server login for the current user is a member of the sysadmin fixed server role.

IF IS_SRVROLEMEMBER ('sysadmin') = 1

print 'Current user"s login is a member of the sysadmin role'

ELSE IF IS_SRVROLEMEMBER ('sysadmin') = 0

print 'Current user"s login is NOT a member of the sysadmin role'

ELSE IF IS_SRVROLEMEMBER ('sysadmin') IS NULL

print 'ERROR: The server role specified is not valid.';

LOGINPROPERTY:
LOGINPROPERTY ('login_name' , 'property_name')

Example: The following example checks whether SQL Server login John3 must change its password the next time it connects to an instance of SQL Server.

SELECT LOGINPROPERTY('John3', 'IsMustChange');

GO

ORIGINAL_LOGIN:
ORIGINAL_LOGIN( )

Example: The following example switches the execution context of the current session from the caller of the statements to login1. The functions SUSER_SNAME and ORIGINAL_LOGIN are used to return the current session user (the user to whom the context was switched), and the original login account.

```
USE AdventureWorks2012;

GO

--Create a temporary login and user.

CREATE LOGIN login1 WITH PASSWORD = 'J345#$)thb';

CREATE USER user1 FOR LOGIN login1;

GO

--Execute a context switch to the temporary login account.

DECLARE @original_login sysname;

DECLARE @current_context sysname;

EXECUTE AS LOGIN = 'login1';

SET @original_login = ORIGINAL_LOGIN();

SET @current_context = SUSER_SNAME();

SELECT 'The current executing context is: '+ @current_context;

SELECT 'The original login in this session was: '+ @original_login
```

GO

-- Return to the original execution context

-- and remove the temporary principal.

REVERT;

GO

DROP LOGIN login1;

DROP USER user1;

GO

PERMISSIONS:

PERMISSIONS ([objectid [, 'column']])

Example: The following example determines whether the current user can execute the CREATE TABLE statement.

IF PERMISSIONS()&2=2

    CREATE TABLE test_table (col1 INT)

ELSE

    PRINT 'ERROR: The current user cannot create a table.';

PWDENCRYPT:

PWDENCRYPT ('password')

PWDCOMPARE:

PWDCOMPARE ('clear_text_password'

, password_hash

[, version])

Example: The following example identifies SQL Server logins that have no passwords.

SELECT name FROM sys.sql_logins

WHERE PWDCOMPARE('', password_hash) = 1 ;

SESSION_USER:

-- Syntax for SQL Server, Azure SQL Database, Azure SQL Data Warehouse, Parallel Data Warehouse

SESSION_USER

Example: The following example creates a table that uses SESSION_USER as a DEFAULT constraint for the name of the person who records receipt of a shipment.

USE AdventureWorks2012;

GO

CREATE TABLE deliveries3

(

order_id int IDENTITY(5000, 1) NOT NULL,

```
cust_id  int NOT NULL,

order_date    smalldatetime    NOT    NULL    DEFAULT
GETDATE(),

delivery_date smalldatetime NOT NULL DEFAULT

DATEADD(dd, 10, GETDATE()),

received_shipment    nchar(30)    NOT    NULL    DEFAULT
SESSION_USER

);

GO
```

Records added to the table will be stamped with the user name of the current user. In this example, Wanida, Sylvester, and Alejandro verify receipt of shipments. This can be emulated by switching user context by using EXECUTE AS.

```
EXECUTE AS USER = 'Wanida'

INSERT deliveries3 (cust_id)

VALUES (7510);

INSERT deliveries3 (cust_id)

VALUES (7231);

REVERT;
```

```
EXECUTE AS USER = 'Sylvester'

INSERT deliveries3 (cust_id)

VALUES (7028);

REVERT;

EXECUTE AS USER = 'Alejandro'

INSERT deliveries3 (cust_id)

VALUES (7392);

INSERT deliveries3 (cust_id)

VALUES (7452);

REVERT;

GO
```

The following query selects all information from the deliveries3 table.

```
SELECT order_id AS 'Order #', cust_id AS 'Customer #',

    delivery_date AS 'When Delivered', received_shipment

    AS 'Received By'

FROM deliveries3

ORDER BY order_id;
```

GO

Resulting in:

Order # Customer # When Delivered Received By

-------- ---------- -------------------- -----------

5000 7510 2005-03-16 12:02:14 Wanida

5001 7231 2005-03-16 12:02:14 Wanida

5002 7028 2005-03-16 12:02:14 Sylvester

5003 7392 2005-03-16 12:02:14 Alejandro

5004 7452 2005-03-16 12:02:14 Alejandro

(5 row(s) affected)

SESSIONPROPERTY:
SESSIONPROPERTY (option)

Example: The following example returns the setting for the CONCAT_NULL_YIELDS_NULL option.

SELECT   SESSIONPROPERTY ('CONCAT_NULL_YIELDS_NULL')

SUSER_ID:
SUSER_ID (['login'])

Example: The following example returns the login identification number for the sa login.

SELECT SUSER_ID('sa');

SUSER_NAME:

SUSER_NAME ([server_user_id])

Example: The following example returns the login identification name of the user with a login identification number of 1.

SELECT SUSER_NAME(1);

SUSER_SID:

SUSER_SID (['login'] [, Param2])

Example: The followng example returns the security identification number (SID) for the current security context.

SELECT SUSER_SID('sa');

SUSER_SNAME:

-- Syntax for SQL Server, Azure SQL Database, Azure SQL Data Warehouse, Parallel Data Warehouse

SUSER_SNAME ([server_user_sid])

Example: The following example uses SUSER_SNAME as a DEFAULT constraint in a CREATE TABLE statement.

USE AdventureWorks2012;

GO

CREATE TABLE sname_example

```
(

login_sname sysname DEFAULT SUSER_SNAME(),

employee_id uniqueidentifier DEFAULT NEWID(),

login_date  datetime DEFAULT GETDATE()

)

GO

INSERT sname_example DEFAULT VALUES;

GO
```

SYSTEM_USER:

-- Syntax for SQL Server, Azure SQL Data Warehouse, Parallel Data Warehouse

```
SYSTEM_USER
```

Example: The following example creates a table with SYSTEM_USER as a DEFAULT constraint for the SRep_tracking_user column.

```
USE AdventureWorks2012;

GO

CREATE TABLE Sales.Sales_Tracking

(
```

```
Territory_id int IDENTITY(2000, 1) NOT NULL,

Rep_id  int NOT NULL,

Last_sale datetime NOT NULL DEFAULT GETDATE(),

SRep_tracking_user  varchar(30)  NOT  NULL  DEFAULT
SYSTEM_USER

)

GO

INSERT Sales.Sales_Tracking (Rep_id)

VALUES (151);

INSERT Sales.Sales_Tracking (Rep_id, Last_sale)

VALUES (293, '19980515');

INSERT Sales.Sales_Tracking (Rep_id, Last_sale)

VALUES (27882, '19980620');

INSERT Sales.Sales_Tracking (Rep_id)

VALUES (21392);

INSERT Sales.Sales_Tracking (Rep_id, Last_sale)

VALUES (24283, '19981130');

GO
```

The following query to selects all the information from the Sales_Tracking table:

SELECT * FROM Sales_Tracking ORDER BY Rep_id;

GO

Results in:

Territory_id Rep_id Last_sale SRep_tracking_user

----------- ------ -------------------- ------------------

2000 151 Mar 4 1998 10:36AM ArvinDak

2001 293 May 15 1998 12:00AM ArvinDak

2003 21392 Mar 4 1998 10:36AM ArvinDak

2004 24283 Nov 3 1998 12:00AM ArvinDak

2002 27882 Jun 20 1998 12:00AM ArvinDak

(5 row(s) affected)

USER:

-- Syntax for SQL Server, Azure SQL Database, Azure SQL Data Warehouse, Parallel Data Warehouse

USER

Example: The following example creates a table by using USER as a DEFAULT constraint for the salesperson of a sales row.

```
USE AdventureWorks2012;

GO

CREATE TABLE inventory22

(

part_id int IDENTITY(100, 1) NOT NULL,

description varchar(30) NOT NULL,

entry_person varchar(30) NOT NULL DEFAULT USER

)

GO

INSERT inventory22 (description)

VALUES ('Red pencil')

INSERT inventory22 (description)

VALUES ('Blue pencil')

INSERT inventory22 (description)

VALUES ('Green pencil')

INSERT inventory22 (description)

VALUES ('Black pencil')

INSERT inventory22 (description)
```

VALUES ('Yellow pencil')

GO

This is the query to select all information from the inventory22 table:

SELECT * FROM inventory22 ORDER BY part_id;

GO

Resulting in:

part_id description entry_person

----------- ------------------------------- -------------------------

100 Red pencil dbo

101 Blue pencil dbo

102 Green pencil dbo

103 Black pencil dbo

104 Yellow pencil dbo

(5 row(s) affected)

USER_ID:
USER_ID (['user'])

Example: The following example returns the identification number for the AdventureWorks2012 user Harold.

```
USE AdventureWorks2012;

SELECT USER_ID('Harold');

GO
```

USER_NAME:

-- Syntax for SQL Server, Azure SQL Database, Azure SQL Data Warehouse, Parallel Data Warehouse

```
USER_NAME ( [ id ] )
```

Example: The following example shows how USER_NAME behaves during impersonation.

```
SELECT USER_NAME();

GO

EXECUTE AS USER = 'Zelig';

GO

SELECT USER_NAME();

GO

REVERT;

GO

SELECT USER_NAME();

GO
```

Resulting in:

DBO

Zelig

DBO

ASCII:

-- Syntax for SQL Server, Azure SQL Database, Azure SQL Data Warehouse, Parallel Data Warehouse

ASCII (character_expression)

Example: The following example assumes an ASCII character set and returns the ASCII value and CHAR character for each character in the string Du monde entier.

SET TEXTSIZE 0;

SET NOCOUNT ON;

-- Create the variables for the current character string position

-- and for the character string.

DECLARE @position int, @string char(15);

-- Initialize the variables.

SET @position = 1;

SET @string = 'Du monde entier';

```
WHILE @position <= DATALENGTH(@string)

  BEGIN

  SELECT ASCII(SUBSTRING(@string, @position, 1)),

    CHAR(ASCII(SUBSTRING(@string, @position, 1)))

   SET @position = @position + 1

  END;

SET NOCOUNT OFF;

GO
```

Resulting in:

```
----------- -

68       D

----------- -

117       u

----------- -

32

----------- -

109       m

----------- -
```

111	o
110	n
100	d
101	e
32	
101	e
110	n
116	t
105	i

101   e

----------- -

114   r

CHAR:

-- Syntax for SQL Server, Azure SQL Database, Azure SQL Data Warehouse, Parallel Data Warehouse

CHAR (integer_expression)

Example: The following example prints the ASCII value and character for each character in the string New Moon.

SET TEXTSIZE 0;

-- Create variables for the character string and for the current

-- position in the string.

DECLARE @position int, @string char(8);

-- Initialize the current position and the string variables.

SET @position = 1;

SET @string = 'New Moon';

WHILE @position <= DATALENGTH(@string)

  BEGIN

  SELECT ASCII(SUBSTRING(@string, @position, 1)),

```
CHAR(ASCII(SUBSTRING(@string, @position, 1)))

    SET @position = @position + 1

    END;

GO

Resulting in:

----------- -

78 N

----------- -

101 e

----------- -

119 w

----------- -

32

----------- -

77 M

----------- -

111 o

----------- -
```

111 o

----------- -

110 n

----------- -

CHARDINEX:

-- Syntax for SQL Server, Azure SQL Database, Azure SQL Data Warehouse, Parallel Data Warehouse

CHARINDEX (expressionToFind , expressionToSearch [, start_location])

Example: The following cxample returns the position at which the sequence of characters bicycle starts in the DocumentSummary column of the Document table in the AdventureWorks2012 database.

DECLARE @document varchar(64);

SELECT @document = 'Reflectors are vital safety' +

' components of your bicycle.';

SELECT CHARINDEX('bicycle', @document);

GO

Resulting in:

48

CONCAT:

-- Syntax for SQL Server, Azure SQL Database, Azure SQL Data Warehouse, Parallel Data Warehouse

CONCAT (string_value1, string_value2 [, string_valueN])

Example:

```
CREATE TABLE #temp (

    emp_name nvarchar(200) NOT NULL,

    emp_middlename nvarchar(200) NULL,

    emp_lastname nvarchar(200) NOT NULL

);

INSERT INTO #temp VALUES( 'Name', NULL, 'Lastname' );

SELECT    CONCAT(    emp_name,    emp_middlename, emp_lastname ) AS Result

FROM #temp;
```

Resulting in:

Result

NameLastname

(1 row(s) affected)

DIFFERENCE:

-- Syntax for SQL Server, Azure SQL Database, Azure SQL Data Warehouse, Parallel Data Warehouse

DIFFERENCE (character_expression , character_expression)

Example: In the first part of the following example, the SOUNDEX values of two very similar strings are compared. For a Latin1_General collation DIFFERENCE returns a value of 4. In the second part of the following example, the SOUNDEX values for two very different strings are compared, and for a Latin1_General collation DIFFERENCE returns a value of 0.

-- Returns a DIFFERENCE value of 4, the least possible difference.

SELECT   SOUNDEX('Green'),   SOUNDEX('Greene'),
DIFFERENCE('Green','Greene');

GO

-- Returns a DIFFERENCE value of 0, the highest possible difference.

SELECT SOUNDEX('Blotchet-Halls'), SOUNDEX('Greene'),
DIFFERENCE('Blotchet-Halls', 'Greene');

GO

Resulting in:

----- ----- -----------

G650 G650 4

(1 row(s) affected)

----- ----- -----------

B432 G650 0

(1 row(s) affected)

FORMAT:

FORMAT (value, format [, culture])

Example:

The following example returns a simple date formatted for different cultures.

DECLARE @d DATETIME = '10/01/2011';

SELECT FORMAT (@d, 'd', 'en-US') AS 'US English Result'

,FORMAT (@d, 'd', 'en-gb') AS 'Great Britain English Result'

,FORMAT (@d, 'd', 'de-de') AS 'German Result'

,FORMAT (@d, 'd', 'zh-cn') AS 'Simplified Chinese (PRC) Result';

SELECT FORMAT (@d, 'D', 'en-US') AS 'US English Result'

,FORMAT (@d, 'D', 'en-gb') AS 'Great Britain English Result'

,FORMAT (@d, 'D', 'de-de') AS 'German Result'

,FORMAT (@d, 'D', 'zh-cn') AS 'Chinese (Simplified PRC) Result';

Resulting in:

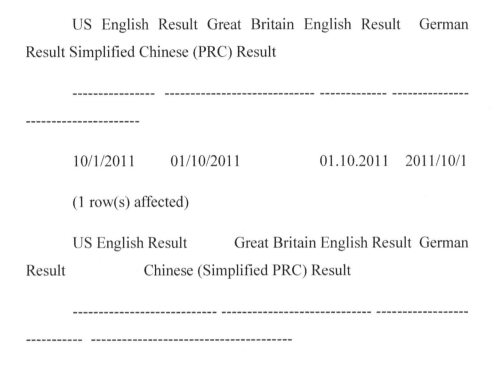

US English Result Great Britain English Result German Result Simplified Chinese (PRC) Result

---------------- ----------------------------- ------------- ---------------

----

10/1/2011   01/10/2011   01.10.2011   2011/10/1

(1 row(s) affected)

US English Result   Great Britain English Result German Result   Chinese (Simplified PRC) Result

-------------------------- ----------------------------- ------------------

----------- ---------------------------------------

Saturday, October 01, 2011   01 October 2011 Samstag, 1. Oktober 2011   2011年10月1日

(1 row(s) affected)

LEFT:

-- Syntax for SQL Server, Azure SQL Database, Azure SQL Data Warehouse, Parallel Data Warehouse

LEFT (character_expression , integer_expression)

Example: The following example returns the five leftmost characters of each product name in the Product table of the AdventureWorks2012 database.

SELECT LEFT(Name, 5)

FROM Production.Product

ORDER BY ProductID;

GO

LEN:

-- Syntax for SQL Server, Azure SQL Database, Azure SQL Data Warehouse, Parallel Data Warehouse

LEN (string_expression)

Example:

The following example selects the number of characters and the data in FirstName for people located in Australia. This example uses the AdventureWorks2012 database.

SELECT LEN(FirstName) AS Length, FirstName, LastName

FROM Sales.vIndividualCustomer

WHERE CountryRegionName = 'Australia';

GO

LOWER:

-- Syntax for SQL Server, Azure SQL Database, Azure SQL Data Warehouse, Parallel Data Warehouse

LOWER (character_expression)

Example:

The following example uses the LOWER function, the UPPER function, and nests the UPPER function inside the LOWER function in selecting product names that have prices between $11 and $20. This example uses the AdventureWorks2012 database.

```
SELECT LOWER(SUBSTRING(Name, 1, 20)) AS Lower,
    UPPER(SUBSTRING(Name, 1, 20)) AS Upper,
    LOWER(UPPER(SUBSTRING(Name, 1, 20))) As LowerUpper
FROM Production.Product
WHERE ListPrice between 11.00 and 20.00;
GO
```

Resulting in:

Lower Upper LowerUpper

-------------------- -------------------- --------------------

minipump MINIPUMP minipump

taillights - battery TAILLIGHTS - BATTERY taillights - battery

(2 row(s) affected)

LTRIM:

-- Syntax for SQL Server, Azure SQL Database, Azure SQL Data Warehouse, Parallel Data Warehouse

LTRIM (character_expression)

Example: The following example uses LTRIM to remove leading spaces from a character variable.

DECLARE @string_to_trim varchar(60);

SET @string_to_trim = '   Five spaces are at the beginning of this

string.';

SELECT 'Here is the string without the leading spaces: ' +

LTRIM(@string_to_trim);

GO

Resulting in:

Here is the string without the leading spaces: Five spaces are at the beginning of this string.

(1 row(s) affected)

NCHAR:

-- Syntax for SQL Server, Azure SQL Database, Azure SQL Data Warehouse, Parallel Data Warehouse

NCHAR (integer_expression)

Example: The following example uses the SUBSTRING, UNICODE, CONVERT, and NCHAR functions to print the character number, the Unicode character, and the UNICODE value of each character in the string København.

-- The @position variable holds the position of the character currently

-- being processed. The @nstring variable is the Unicode character

-- string to process.

DECLARE @position int, @nstring nchar(9);

-- Initialize the current position variable to the first character in

-- the string.

SET @position = 1;

-- Initialize the character string variable to the string to process.

-- Notice that there is an N before the start of the string. This

-- indicates that the data following the N is Unicode data.

```sql
SET @nstring = N'København';
```

-- Print the character number of the position of the string you are at,

-- the actual Unicode character you are processing, and the UNICODE

-- value for this particular character.

```sql
PRINT 'Character #' + ' ' + 'Unicode Character' + ' ' + 'UNICODE Value';

WHILE @position <= DATALENGTH(@nstring)

  BEGIN

  SELECT @position,

    NCHAR(UNICODE(SUBSTRING(@nstring,   @position, 1))),

    CONVERT(NCHAR(17),        SUBSTRING(@nstring, @position, 1)),

    UNICODE(SUBSTRING(@nstring, @position, 1))

  SELECT @position = @position + 1

  END;
```

GO

Resulting in:

Character # Unicode Character UNICODE Value

----------- ---- ----------------- -----------

1   K   K   75

(1 row(s) affected)

----------- ---- ----------------- -----------

2   ø   ø   248

(1 row(s) affected)

----------- ---- ----------------- -----------

3   b   b   98

(1 row(s) affected)

----------- ---- ----------------- -----------

4   e   e   101

(1 row(s) affected)

----------- ---- ----------------- -----------

5   n   n   110

(1 row(s) affected)

```
----------- ---- ----------------- -----------
6       h   h           104
```

(1 row(s) affected)

```
----------- ---- ----------------- -----------
7       a   a           97
```

(1 row(s) affected)

```
----------- ---- ----------------- -----------
8       v   v           118
```

(1 row(s) affected)

```
----------- ---- ----------------- -----------
9       n   n           110
```

(1 row(s) affected)

```
----------- ---- ----------------- -----------
10      NULL            NULL
```

(1 row(s) affected)

```
----------- ---- ----------------- -----------
11      NULL            NULL
```

(1 row(s) affected)

----------- ---- ---------------- -----------

12   NULL   NULL

(1 row(s) affected)

----------- ---- ---------------- -----------

13   NULL   NULL

(1 row(s) affected)

----------- ---- ---------------- -----------

14   NULL   NULL

(1 row(s) affected)

----------- ---- ---------------- -----------

15   NULL   NULL

(1 row(s) affected)

----------- ---- ---------------- -----------

16   NULL   NULL

(1 row(s) affected)

----------- ---- ---------------- -----------

17   NULL   NULL

(1 row(s) affected)

```
------------ ---- ----------------- -----------

18        NULL            NULL
```

(1 row(s) affected)

PATINDEX:
-- Syntax for SQL Server, Azure SQL Database, Azure SQL Data Warehouse, Parallel Data Warehouse

PATINDEX ('%pattern%' , expression)

Example: The following example checks a short character string (interesting data) for the starting location of the characters ter.

SELECT PATINDEX('%ter%', 'interesting data');

Resulting in:

3

QUOTENAME:
-- Syntax for SQL Server, Azure SQL Database, Azure SQL Data Warehouse, Parallel Data Warehouse

QUOTENAME ('character_string' [, 'quote_character'])

Example: The following example takes the character string abc[]def and uses the [and] characters to create a valid SQL Server delimited identifier.

SELECT QUOTENAME('abc[]def');

Resulting in:

[abc[]]def]

(1 row(s) affected)

REPLACE:

-- Syntax for SQL Server, Azure SQL Database, Azure SQL Data Warehouse, Parallel Data Warehouse

REPLACE (string_expression , string_pattern , string_replacement)

Examples:

The following example replaces the string cde in abcdefghi with xxx.

SELECT REPLACE('abcdefghicde','cde','xxx');

GO

Resulting in:

----

abxxxfghixxx

(1 row(s) affected)

REPLICATE:

-- Syntax for SQL Server, Azure SQL Database, Azure SQL Data Warehouse, Parallel Data Warehouse

REPLICATE (string_expression ,integer_expression)

Example:

The following example replicates a 0 character four times in front of a production line code in the AdventureWorks2012 database.

SELECT [Name]

, REPLICATE('0', 4) + [ProductLine] AS 'Line Code'

FROM [Production].[Product]

WHERE [ProductLine] = 'T'

ORDER BY [Name];

GO

Results in:

Name	Line Code
HL Touring Frame - Blue, 46	0000T
HL Touring Frame - Blue, 50	0000T
HL Touring Frame - Blue, 54	0000T
HL Touring Frame - Blue, 60	0000T
HL Touring Frame - Yellow, 46	0000T

HL Touring Frame - Yellow, 50   0000T

...

REVERSE:

-- Syntax for SQL Server, Azure SQL Database, Azure SQL Data Warehouse, Parallel Data Warehouse

REVERSE (string_expression)

Example: The following example returns all contact first names with the characters reversed. This example uses the AdventureWorks2012 database.

SELECT FirstName, REVERSE(FirstName) AS Reverse

FROM Person.Person

WHERE BusinessEntityID < 5

ORDER BY FirstName;

GO

Results in:

FirstName Reverse

-------------- --------------

Ken neK

Rob boR

Roberto otreboR

Terri irreT

(4 row(s) affected)

RIGHT:

-- Syntax for SQL Server, Azure SQL Database, Azure SQL Data Warehouse, Parallel Data Warehouse

RIGHT (character_expression , integer_expression)

Example: The following example returns the five rightmost characters of the first name for each person in the AdventureWorks2012 database.

```
SELECT RIGHT(FirstName, 5) AS 'First Name'

FROM Person.Person

WHERE BusinessEntityID < 5

ORDER BY FirstName;

GO
```

Resulting in:

First Name

Ken

Terri

berto

Rob

(4 row(s) affected)

RTRIM:

-- Syntax for SQL Server, Azure SQL Database, Azure SQL Data Warehouse, Parallel Data Warehouse

RTRIM (character_expression)

Example: The following example demonstrates how to use RTRIM to remove trailing spaces from a character variable.

DECLARE @string_to_trim varchar(60);

SET @string_to_trim = 'Four spaces are after the period in this sentence.   ';

SELECT @string_to_trim + ' Next string.';

SELECT RTRIM(@string_to_trim) + ' Next string.';

GO

Resulting in:

Four spaces are after the period in this sentence. Next string.

(1 row(s) affected)

Four spaces are after the period in this sentence. Next string.

(1 row(s) affected)

SOUNDEX:
-- Syntax for SQL Server, Azure SQL Database, Azure SQL Data Warehouse, Parallel Data Warehouse

SOUNDEX (character_expression)

Example:

The following example shows the SOUNDEX function and the related DIFFERENCE function. In the first example, the standard SOUNDEX values are returned for all consonants. Returning the SOUNDEX for Smith and Smythe returns the same SOUNDEX result because all vowels, the letter y, doubled letters, and the letter h, are not included.

-- Using SOUNDEX

SELECT SOUNDEX ('Smith'), SOUNDEX ('Smythe');

Resulting in:

----- -----

S530 S530

(1 row(s) affected)

SPACE:

-- Syntax for SQL Server, Azure SQL Database, Azure SQL Data Warehouse, Parallel Data Warehouse

SPACE (integer_expression)

Examples:

The following example trims the last names and concatenates a comma, two spaces, and the first names of people listed in the Person table in AdventureWorks2012.

USE AdventureWorks2012;

GO

SELECT RTRIM(LastName) + ',' + SPACE(2) + LTRIM(FirstName)

FROM Person.Person

ORDER BY LastName, FirstName;

GO

STR:

-- Syntax for SQL Server, Azure SQL Database, Azure SQL Data Warehouse, Parallel Data Warehouse

STR (float_expression [, length [, decimal]])

Example: The following example converts an expression that is made up of five digits and a decimal point to a six-position character string. The fractional part of the number is rounded to one decimal place.

SELECT STR(123.45, 6, 1);

GO

Resulting in:

123.5

(1 row(s) affected)

STRING_ESCAPE:
STRING_ESCAPE(text , type)

Example:

The following query creates JSON text from number and string variables, and escapes any special JSON character in variables.

SET @json = FORMATMESSAGE('{ "id": %d,"name": "%s", "surname": "%s" }',

17,   STRING_ESCAPE(@name,'json'), STRING_ESCAPE(@surname,'json'));

STRING_SPLIT:
STRING_SPLIT (string , separator)

Example: Parse a comma separated list of values and return all non-empty tokens:

DECLARE @tags NVARCHAR(400) = 'clothing,road,,touring,bike'

SELECT value

FROM STRING_SPLIT(@tags, ',')

WHERE RTRIM(value) <> '';

STRING_SPLIT will return empty string if there is nothing between separator. Condition RTRIM(value) <> '' will remove empty tokens.

STUFF:

-- Syntax for SQL Server, Azure SQL Database, Azure SQL Data Warehouse, Parallel Data Warehouse

STUFF (character_expression , start , length , replaceWith_expression)

*All tables and coding referenced from Microsoft. (Microsoft, 2012)

With that, we come to the end of scalar functions. Do not forget to go through the functions again so as to make sure that you have understood them properly. It will take time for you to utilize them in the best manner when you are working on SQL. You can always refer back to the list whenever you are using scalar functions.

CHAPTER 6

CREATING A TABLE IN SQL

The table is at the crux of SQL. Tables organize the data. Any work that you do in SQL will ultimately be related to a table or the other. As such, it is essential that you understand how to create a table as soon as possible. We shall be taking a look at this in this chapter.

In order to create a simple table, you need to name the table and then define the columns. You will also have to define the data type of each of those columns.

CREATE TABLE statement

In order to make a new table, you will have to make use of the CREATE TABLE statement. For using this statement, you can refer to the following syntax.

CREATE TABLE table_name(

column1 datatype,

column2 datatype,

column3 datatype,

.....

columnN datatype,

PRIMARY KEY(one or more columns)

);

The database system needs to be told what you wish to do with the help of a keyword. For creating a new table, you need the keyword, CREATE TABLE. This statement will be followed by an identifier or a unique name which will be used to identify this table.

As you can see in the example, you will notice that there is a list present inside the brackets. The list will define each of the columns present in the table. It will also inform the system about the data type of each column.

Creating a Table

To properly understand how a table is created in SQL, take a look at the example given below. In the following example, a CUSTOMERS table is created. The primary key for the table is ID in this example. The table also features the constraint, NOT NULL. As a result, it is not possible for the fields to have a NULL value.

SQL> CREATE TABLE CUSTOMERS(

ID   INT   NOT NULL,

NAME VARCHAR (20)   NOT NULL,

AGE   INT   NOT NULL,

ADDRESS   CHAR (25) ,

SALARY   DECIMAL (18, 2),

PRIMARY KEY (ID)

);

It is possible to verify that the table has been created successfully in an easy manner. You simply need to check the message displayed by SQL. Alternatively, you can make use of the DESC command as shown below.

SQL> DESC CUSTOMERS;

```
+---------+---------------+------+-----+---------+-------+
| Field   | Type          | Null | Key | Default | Extra |
+---------+---------------+------+-----+---------+-------+
| ID      | int(11)       | NO   | PRI |         |       |
| NAME    | varchar(20)   | NO   |     |         |       |
| AGE     | int(11)       | NO   |     |         |       |
| ADDRESS | char(25)      | YES  |     | NULL    |       |
| SALARY  | decimal(18,2) | YES  |     | NULL    |       |
+---------+---------------+------+-----+---------+-------+
```

5 rows in set (0.00 sec)

Congratulations! Your database now has a table named DESC CUSTOMERS. Now, get started and practice creating tables. Try out the functions that you have learned so that you become stronger in SQL.

CHAPTER 7

RECOMMENDATIONS

Amazon is an amazing resource for anyone looking to purchase or sell items on the internet. When it comes to learning about new things, Amazon is an incredible resource for anyone looking to expand their knowledge.

When it comes to sitting at the computer, specifically when we you work on a computer all day, there are certain risks that go along with the profession. Regular hand exercises are crucial in preventing the development of carpal tunnel and unnecessary joint stress. An item by Koh Fit called Stress Ball Hand Exerciser. This item is rated by nearly 200 people and has an average of five out of five stars.

This is a great product to not only exercise your hands but also provide you with a booklet on physical therapy and taking better care of your muscles. You can also use the exercise ball as a stress ball to relieve tension when things become stressful at work. The set is priced at $10.99.

Although SQL involves mostly online work, there will come a time when you need to take notes, write down certain functions and statements that you need to remember but are having difficulty remembering. AmazonBasics sells a 12 pack of writing pads,

"AmazonBasics 8-1/2 by 11-3/4 Legal Pad – White, this pad contains 50 sheets per pad, with a four and a half out of five stars and over 400 reviews. These legal, white pads are priced at $9.99 for 12 writing pads.

If you desire to fix your computer or build a new computer, there is a highly-rated tool kit on Amazon that is specifically described as a computer based tool kit. The product is sold by Rosewill and have over 1,000 reviews averaging at four and a half out of five stars. The description is named as Rosewill 90 Piece Professional Computer Tool Kit Component's Other RTK-090 Black. The price of the tool kit is set at $22.99.

A lot of people who work from home either sit at their table, their kitchen countertop, their sofa, their bed, etc. Having a computer desk is essential in working efficiently, effectively, and keeping organized. Amazon sells a wonderful desk by Altra Furniture, "Altra Dakota L-Shaped Desk with Bookshelves, Dark Russet Cherry". The desk is priced at $77.88 with nearly 2,000 reviews averaging at four out of five stars.

CONCLUSION

Although this book is essential and encompasses nearly every aspect of the SQL language, this book doesn't cover nearly everything you need to know about SQL. Should you desire to learn more about the language, there are numerous other sources of information available to the public, free of charge. This book can serve as a guide to learning the language and a quick reference in the future.

I hope that you enjoyed this book and that you took something useful from it.

Do leave a review to let me know what you thought of this book and what, if anything, you would like me to add to it.

WORKS CITED

3C Schools. (2015, May 4). *3C Schools*. Retrieved from SQL Quick Reference From W3Schools: http://www.w3c-schools.com/sql/sql_quickref.asp.htm

Microsoft. (2008, October 16). *GROUPING_ID (Transact-SQL)* . Retrieved from Microsoft: https://msdn.microsoft.com/en-us/library/bb510624.aspx

Microsoft. (2010, July 21). *AVG (Transact-SQL)* . Retrieved from Microsoft: https://msdn.microsoft.com/en-us/library/ms177677.aspx

Microsoft. (2012, February 9). *SCOPE_IDENTITY (Transact-SQL)*. Retrieved from Microsoft TechNet: https://technet.microsoft.com/en-us/library/ms190315(v=sql.110).aspx

Microsoft. (2012, January 6). *SYSTEM_USER (Transact-SQL)*. Retrieved from Microsoft TechNet: https://technet.microsoft.com/en-us/library/ms179930(v=sql.110).aspx

Microsoft. (2014, October 21). *INDEX_COL (Transact-SQL)*. Retrieved from Microsoft Developer Network: https://msdn.microsoft.com/en-us/library/ms178545.aspx

Microsoft. (2016, September 28). *Deterministic and Nondeterministic Functions.* Retrieved from Microsoft: https://msdn.microsoft.com/en-us/library/ms178091.aspx

Microsoft. (2016, June 2). *JSON_VALUE (Transact-SQL).* Retrieved from Microsoft Developer Network: https://msdn.microsoft.com/en-us/library/dn921898.aspx

SQL Course.com. (2016, September 1). *Creating Tables.* Retrieved from SQL Course : http://www.sqlcourse.com/create.html

Stack Overflow. (2015, March 11). *Difference between HAVING and WHERE clause in SQL [duplicate].* Retrieved from Stack Overflow: http://stackoverflow.com/questions/7383881/difference-between-having-and-where-clause-in-sql

w3schools. (2016, August 2). *SQL Data Types for Various DBs.* Retrieved from w3schools: http://www.w3schools.com/sql/sql_datatypes.asp

Who Is Hosting This? (2016, August 1). *Database Administration-ANSI SQL Standards and Guidelines.* Retrieved from Who Is Hosting This?: http://www.whoishostingthis.com/resources/ansi-sql-standards/

Made in the
USA
Monee, IL